London 1900

LONDON 1900

Alastair Service

RIZZOLI
NEW YORK

Published in the United States of America
in 1979 by:

Rizzoli INTERNATIONAL PUBLICATIONS, INC.
712 Fifth Avenue/New York 10019

Library of Congress Catalog Card Number: 78–68491
ISBN: 0–8478–0214–0

Published in Great Britain by Granada Publishing
in Crosby Lockwood Staples 1979

*Printed and bound at William Clowes & Sons Limited
Beccles and London*

Contents

Figure Acknowledgements

The author wishes to thank the following for providing the illustrations listed.

André Goulancourt: frontispiece photograph.

Mansell Collection: Figures 1, 14, 22, 65, 67, 69, 71, 107, 114, 124, 140, 155, 166, 183, 193, 227, 228, 229, 230, 231.

National Monuments Record, Copyright Watney Mann Group: Figures 3, 63, 64, 116.

National Monuments Record, Crown Copyright: Figures 5, 10, 11, 13, 23, 48, 54, 55, 58, 59, 70, 72, 82, 85, 86, 87, 88, 93, 94, 96, 102, 104, 105, 108, 110, 111, 112, 113, 115, 117, 120, 123, 125, 126, 127, 129, 130, 131, 132, 135, 136, 137, 138, 154, 160, 161, 172, 173, 174, 175, 180, 181, 184, 189, 195, 196, 197, 198, 199, 202, 204, 205, 207, 210, 214, 215, 217, 219, 220, 221, 224, 225.

A. F. Kersting: Figure 7.

National Monuments Record, Copyright B. T. Batsford: Figures 98, 213.

Architectural Press: Figure 99.

Harrods Limited: Figure 103.

Mewès & Davis: Figure 139.

Broadway Church Action: Figure 151.

William Toomey: Figures 163, 222.

National Monuments Record, Copyright N. Cooper: Figure 218.

The following photographs were taken by the author: Figures 8, 9, 17, 18, 19, 20, 21, 25, 27, 28, 30, 31, 32, 33, 34, 35, 40, 45, 46, 47, 49, 51, 52, 57, 62, 68, 73, 75, 76, 77, 78, 79, 80, 81, 84, 89, 90, 95, 100, 106, 109, 119, 121, 122, 141, 142, 143, 146, 148, 149, 150, 156, 158, 159, 164, 167, 169, 171, 176, 177, 179, 182, 185, 186, 187, 188, 191, 192, 194, 200, 206, 208, 211, 226.

All photographs not in the above lists are from the author's own collection.

Dedicated to Louisa

Preface and Acknowledgements

Many of the world's great cities still owe a great deal of their visual character to the buildings put up in the years around 1900. Paris, Glasgow, Vienna, Barcelona, Cape Town, Chicago and Brussels come to mind as examples. But London – from Whitehall to Oxford Street and Knightsbridge, from the Mall and Piccadilly to suburbs such as Barnes or Golders Green – takes its flavour from its late Victorian and Edwardian buildings to an extraordinary degree.

The architectural styles of those buildings of about 1900 vary confusingly. Byzantine, Romanesque, Gothic, Tudor, Renaissance, various forms of Classicism and Baroque – all these appear, as well as mixtures of styles and attempts at new styles. Thus the architectural historian's traditional approach to a period, tracing the development of structure and style, would give very little understanding of the splendid London buildings of the turn of the century. Instead, this book examines the architecture in chapters based on types and functions of building – houses, theatres, pubs, town halls and so on – setting each type against the relevant social, political and economic history of London at a time when its people and their institutions were undergoing dramatic changes in many ways.

In the space available for the text in a book largely dependent on illustrations of these people and their buildings, it is only possible to give an outline of the main events lying behind each type of design. But it is enough to show the fascination of the far-reaching social developments which caused the buildings to be erected and which made widely varying architectural expression acceptable to the clients involved.

I owe much to a great many people who have helped me with the book. Dennis Sharp suggested the book to me in the first place. The form it has taken owes much to discussions I have had with him and with Gavin Stamp (who was organising an excellent RIBA exhibition on London 1900 buildings at the time I was writing the book), while the relevance and interest of the social and economic background was first urged on me by Andrew Saint. I have been fortunate in receiving many suggestions from Michael Robbins, the historian of London's transport, and from Roderick Gradidge, whose questing mind has shown many new viewpoints on the design history of the period. Nicholas Cooper and others at the photographic collection of the National Monuments Record have given me valuable assistance in finding illustrations. Robert Thorne kindly commented on some chapters and gave detailed information from London records to which access is otherwise difficult. Andrew Saint also kindly read the manuscript and suggested numerous points of detail and of interpretation, most of which I have gratefully adopted. Information has also been given by Dorothy Reynolds, Ben Weinreb, Richard Woollard, Margaret Richardson, Lynne Walker, Lynda Fairbairn, Hermione Hobhouse, Victor Glasstone, Susan Beattie, Vanessa Debenham, A. S. Gray (whose Biographical Dictionary of Edwardian Architects is eagerly awaited) and others including the late and lamented Jim Dyos, whose social history of London at the end of the century was sadly uncompleted. All of us owe a great deal in many different ways to Sir Nikolaus Pevsner, Sir John Summerson and Sir John Betjeman. Jean Bradbery provided me with the isolated space in which to write the book and with much encouragement, and John Thackara and Susan Justice have been most helpful editors. The staff of the London Library and the library of the Royal Institute of British Architects have given patient assistance. I am extremely grateful to them all.

The buildings mentioned in the book are usually given two dates, e.g. 1900–03, in which case the first is the date of design (where known) and the second of the completion of the building. Where one date only is given, the building was designed and completed within one year, as is common enough for houses, or only one year has been established.

Alastair Service

1 Imperial Capital 1900

London in 1900 was a city obsessed with a far-away war. *The Times*, London's leading newspaper, reflected the obsession in its New Year's Day editorial.[1]

> The New Year, the last of the Nineteenth Century, which begins today, is not unlikely to mark a turning point in the history of the British Empire. Two important tasks lie before us ... to bring the war in South Africa to a speedy and successful end and ... to review the history of the campaign, to draw from it its true lessons ... Our military system has been tried and it has been found wanting.

Only three years earlier the country had celebrated Queen Victoria's Diamond Jubilee, sixty years' reign by the Queen and Empress over the most extensive empire the world had ever seen. And then, in 1899, its citizens were outraged to find that the poor Dutch farmers in South Africa could defy and beat the British army in the field in the pursuit of their own interests. By the start of 1900, British settlements such as Ladysmith and Kimberley were under siege. On New Year's Day the Queen received a telegram which typifies the attitudes of the time. 'The inhabitants of Kimberley send your Majesty New Year's greetings. The trouble they have passed through and are still enduring only tends to love and loyalty towards your Majesty's throne and person.'[2] Londoners, like other Britishers, reacted to the distant war with a new nationalistic feeling which spread among all but the poorest classes. The same issue of *The Times* reported, 'The Lord Mayor and Sheriffs will go in state to the Guildhall this morning to witness the enrolment of the first 500 selected men of the City of London Imperial Volunteers.' Crowds of people gathered in the streets to give their moral support to the new recruits for the war which was to continue until 1902, although the City Volunteers returned to a triumphant reception in London in November 1900.

All this may seem to have no immediate connection with the architecture of 1900. But these events were important to contemporary builders and architects, and to the people for whom the buildings were erected. Consideration of these and other preoccupations of the period will increase understanding of the new designs. The streets through which such processions passed were to change a great deal at the turn of the century and during the next decade. Road surfaces in central London started to get smoother, street lighting brighter and remaining pockets of slum hovels disappeared. It is good to remember that, although many pretty Georgian houses disappeared in the demolition and rebuilding of the Edwardian decade which started the twentieth century, most of the buildings destroyed were disease-ridden and built of wretched materials.

On the pavements and in the roads, central London in 1900 offered an abundance of contrasts. One writer, looking back at that time, thirty years later, recorded

Fig. 1 November 1900. The return of the City of London Imperial Volunteers from the Boer War in South Africa. The procession in Hyde Park.

A London of horse-trams with halfpenny fares, and of hansom cabs; of crystalline bells and spattering hoofs. A London with winters of slush and fog of a richer sort than any known today, and summers of dust and clam; the slush and the dust being its heritage from the horse-traffic. A London of silk hats, frock-coats, beards, curled moustaches, choker collars, leg-of-mutton sleeves, veils, bonnets and, threading through these gigmanities as herald of revolt, an execrated vixen in bloomers riding a bicycle. A London of solid homes, which regarded the introduction of flat-life as something Not Quite Nice ... A London of low buildings ... of lost corners; of queer nooks and rookeries (slums of little jerry-built houses with only narrow alleys between them); of curling lanes and derelict squares ... A London which, away from the larger streets, held pools of utter darkness and terraces of crumbling caverns ... A London whose roads were mainly granite setts, and therefore a London of turmoil and clatter. A London which was the centre of an empire and knew it. And a London which, in a few of its nerves, was beginning to be aware of the end of an epoch and of the new this and the new that.[3]

Fig. 2   Traffic in the Strand, *c.*1900.

The new this and the new that were far-reaching in their effects on the city and its inhabitants, and the writer was right to imply that it would have been hard to foresee which of these developments were going to become lasting factors in twentieth century life. The population of London and its inner suburbs, the area governed by the London County Council created in 1889, reached its census peak of 4 546 000 in 1901 and then started the long dispersal of its inhabitants which left only 2 723 000 in those parts of the capital by 1971.[4] Greater London, on the other hand, continued to experience the rapid population growth which it had known all through the nineteenth century, as people moved from the inner to the new outer suburbs. In outline and in rounded figures, the population of Greater London was 1 100 000 in 1801; 2 700 000 in 1851; 5 600 000 in 1891; 6 600 000 in 1901; 7 300 000 in 1911 and 8 200 000 in 1931.[5] The reason for this outward growth of suburbs was largely the

Fig. 3   Lant Street, Borough in the 1890s.

arrival of quick electric public transport (see chapters four and six) enabling the outer suburban dweller to commute to central London in an acceptable time. The first lengthy electric underground railway opened in 1900 and electric trams ran in 1901, while the combustion engine soon followed with the first motor buses in 1905.

Faster forms of transport coincided with an increase in the number of adequately paid jobs due to increasing recruitment by government and commerce as both extended their activities immensely at a time of low prices and rising wages. In 1881 109 000 people were employed in public administration; by 1911 there were 271 000. And the people suited to these clerical jobs now existed, thanks to improvements in London schools and education in the last third of the nineteenth century.

The whole structure of employment in Britain changed strikingly during the second half of the nineteenth century. Despite the Industrial Revolution about a quarter of all men in Britain worked on the land in various forms of employment in 1851, while the census of that year showed that one man in every six was a farm labourer. During the 1870s, cheap food flowing into England from the newly developing colonies, and elsewhere, effectively ruined British agriculture for thirty years. Workmen and their families flowed into the towns and cities, especially London, seeking jobs in the manufacturing industries and swelling the slums. By 1881, only one man in ten was an agricultural labourer and by 1911 only one man in twenty.[6] After 1881, the actual *numbers* of farm labourers (as against their proportion of the total) remained almost steady, so it was new industrial and clerical jobs for the increasing town-reared population which caused the changes in these statistics, rather than further migration to the towns on a large scale.

British manufacturing industry, having been the first in the world to develop on a large scale in the period around 1800, was old-fashioned by 1900, suffering from outdated machinery and insufficient capital redevelopment. English shareholders' profits transformed into capital towards the end of the century were mostly invested in developing countries, rather than in home industry. It was only the expansion of the world demand for manufactured goods which enabled many industries to continue to prosper during the end of Queen Victoria's reign and the start of King Edward VII's in 1901–10. With electricity and the oil-powered combustion engine came new industries, which developed strongly after 1910. But in 1900 these were just starting to appear on a small scale, the reconnaissance units of the industrial age's second wave.

All these factors contributed to the general economic situation as it affected ordinary Londoners in 1900. The prices of goods of all sorts had risen rapidly through a succession of strong booms and smaller depressions from 1851, the year of the Great Exhibition, until the major boom of 1868–73. This was followed by a long period of falling prices, with only weak booms and some alarming slumps, until 1896 when a new boom started a long period of rising prices. At first these price increases were slow, but the trend became faster after 1905. The booms of this period came in 1900, 1907 and 1913[7]–a fact worth remembering in considering the new buildings of the time, for that industry was affected although its peaks and troughs did not coincide with those of the national economy. A building boom ran on from 1897 until 1906, despite a depression in town house construction after 1899. The trade prospered again during the turbulent years of 1910–14. Another important point to note is that the period of declining prices up to the late 1890s coincided with an all round increase in the levels of wages, so that many people really were a great deal better off by 1900. Moreover, there is a time-lag between the year when a long-term trend sets in and the years when it is felt by ordinary people. Thus it was almost the year of King Edward's death, 1910, before the higher prices started to pinch the families who had benefited from the long earlier period of rising pay. There was good reason, therefore, for many such people to develop the myth of the golden Edwardian era which is still widespread today.

The people who benefited least during these years were some members of the manual labouring classes, and the poor slum dwellers who could find no adequately paid labour. The slums of London and other major cities seemed a problem of Augean size to more fortunate Englishmen of conscience in 1900. Parliament had been conscious of the need for action throughout the second half of the nineteenth century and Act after Act had been passed.[8] Indeed, a great deal of improvement was achieved during that time, but not enough.

During the debates in the House of Commons on the *Housing of the Working Classes Act* of 1900, which enabled Local Authorities to buy land for housing schemes beyond their own geographical boundaries, Mr Balfour complained that so many M.P.s' speeches had

> dilated on the actual fact of overcrowding, which is admitted by everyone. Workmen and their families do not wish to live in solitary blocks planted in bare fields outside the towns ... Yet if something in the nature of small settlements can be formed ... within easy reach, by locomotion, of the city work, they will still help to relieve the present pressure ... The evil of overcrowding will not be ended yet. The difficulty is too complex, the solutions too numerous[9].

Fig. 4   London children in the park dressed in their Sunday best, *c*.1900.

It was in 1900 that a new Architect, W. E. Riley, was appointed to the London County Council. Riley was no designer but he was a master of organised building programmes. It was from that year on that the big L.C.C. housing estates started to reach completion in large quantities, changing the lives of many thousands of people. Other social changes too were just starting to be felt. Women were beginning to emerge from their traditional Victorian family, social and domestic roles into wider fields of work. Working class women were increasingly employed in the factories of various types of light industry. Among the upper middle classes, a new breed – female interior decorators – suddenly emerged in the 1890s[10] in London. After 1905, women were increasingly employed as clerks and typists in the business offices of the City and the West End, partly because the custom of the time permitted employers to pay them much less than men. By 1910, this trend was making it more difficult to find domestic maids at the even lower wages which could be afforded by middle-class householders,[11] creating another well-founded popular myth about the golden Edwardian age before the 'servant problem'. We can visualise a neat, though oversimplified, image[12] of the recognisable types of girls seen in London around 1900.

> You could immediately recognise the social girl, the middle-class girl, the City girl and the factory girl ... The factory girl wore a black straw hat, ear-rings, a 'Mizpah' brooch, and hair dressed in rolls over her ears. The City girl was neat and severe. The middle-class girl was also neat, but added a touch of the style and chic which in those days could only be had by money. The society girl was consciously and demonstrably the society girl.

One of the results of this widening of the activities open to women, together with the new if conflicting consciousness of their status brought about by publicity for the Suffrage movement of the 1900s, was a reduction in the average family size and hence in population growth. This was made possible by early forms of birth control, but it would not have taken place without far deeper changes of social attitude among the British people brought about by a decline in the influence of the conservative churches on social behaviour and by improvements in public health and hygiene which brought the death rate and the infant mortality rate down sharply.

Such profound changes in accepted ideas can be found in many fields of British life at the start of the twentieth century. The rise of the influence of trades unions (see chapter seven) and the arrival of the first Independent Labour Party M.P.s at Westminster were to alter the whole aspect of British politics. The nineteenth century concern for the well-being of the poor, demonstrated by the activities and inventive architecture of numerous Christian charities in the London slums (see chapter thirteen), found general acceptance in the increasing adoption of the theories of Collectivism by central and local government – almost unnoticed, government accepted wider responsibility for improving the lives of the deprived classes, exceeding even the most extreme proposals made by Jeremy Bentham and Edwin Chadwick in the early nineteenth century. The great town halls and Whitehall government buildings dating from about 1900 were a direct result of these changing ideas and fields of action, for the implementation of Collectivism entailed a vast new staff for the civil service. Housing estates, fire stations, swimming pools, police stations and schools appeared in London at an unprecedented rate, all financed by ratepayers and taxpayers.

It was this sort of government activity, notably in slum clearance and rehousing, which lay behind most of the major rebuilding projects which took place in central London in Edwardian times, combined with older notions of civic pride in the capital city. Throughout the nineteenth century, the vision of major avenues and thoroughfares – initiated by Nash's Regent Street and even earlier – had gradually been realised in London. Victoria Street in Westminster was constructed in 1845–51, followed by an even greater if less visible undertaking, the London main sewerage system started in 1859. The Victoria Embankment dates from 1864 to 1870 and Queen Victoria Street in the City from 1867 to 1871. After that a start was made on Northumberland Avenue in 1874 across the site of Northumberland House, while Shaftesbury Avenue and Charing Cross Road cut through networks of little streets. Compared with the monumental scale of these schemes, most of the avenue-building of Edwardian times in London was on a modest scale; the widening of the Strand from 1899 onwards and the building of Millbank through the Thames-side slums of Westminster to the Tate Gallery in 1901–13 were among the major works. Whitehall, Parliament Square and The Mall were radically changed by new buildings at this time. But the project which most caught the public imagination in 1900 was the new main street from the Strand to Holborn with an extension on to Russell Square.

This avenue, Kingsway, with the crescent of the Aldwych at its southern end, was the pride of the young London County Council, which directed a committee to make plans soon after its own creation in 1889. The plan was published in 1898 and demolition of the infamous rookery on the site started in August 1900. Countless suggestions were made about the style to be adopted in the buildings that would grow along it and about the name of the street itself. One proposal was that it should be called 'Gordon Avenue, in commemoration of the noblest Englishman of our time'.[13] But Kingsway won the day, and King Edward duly carried out the opening ceremony in October 1905. The new street ran above a subterranean passage to enable the L.C.C.'s new electric trams to rise from the Embankment to the road level at the northern end. The building sites along the thoroughfare were sold slowly and the road still stood naked by the time the King, for whom it was named, died in 1910.[14]

By that time, another great urban redevelopment was in hand which was to cause even more controversy. This was the rebuilding of all the houses of Regent Street, involving the demolition of many buildings in stucco (a material much despised by the Edwardians) by Neo-Classical masters such as Sir John Soane, C. R. Cockerell and John Nash. The designs for the block to replace one side of Nash's curving Quadrant section were prepared in 1905 by Norman Shaw, but only the Piccadilly Hotel part (opened in 1908) was built. Long wrangles between shopkeepers and the authorities about the areas of glass provided for street windows led to a new design for the rest by Sir Reginald Blomfield and completion was delayed until 1930.[15]

Looking back at 1900, we may regret the destruction of Regent Street as Nash knew it and even of the vernacular timber houses which crowded the riverside where Millbank now lies. But to an Edwardian it was evident that most of the big redevelopments were much needed.

> That London was not only a London of mud, but a London of darker nights ... Away from the principal streets it was none too well lit. There were miles of sad streets, heavy houses and small glimmering shops. One of the terrors of my childhood was those long silent side-streets, with only a sickly lamp here and there, stretching into an infinity of murk and pathos ... One turned from them to the light and movement of the main streets as to a sanctuary.[16]

Fig. 5 (*Following page*)   The Aldwych and the bottom of Kingsway in late Edwardian years. Inveresk House on the left (offices for the *Morning Post* newspaper) by Mewès and Davis (1906–07) and the Gaiety Theatre by Norman Shaw (1901–03, demolished *c.*1950), with the Waldorf Hotel by A. Marshall Mackenzie and Son (1906) in the background.

2 Architects, Styles and Building Materials

The general approach taken in this book to the architecture and design of the late nineteenth and early twentieth centuries is to examine the buildings according to their function, setting them in the context of the relevant historical situation and general ideas about their use. Only by seeing the architecture against this background can we explain the otherwise bewildering variety of styles that architects of the time saw fit to use in designing these buildings, which were usually impressive and often beautiful. Before embarking on the examination of the different types of buildings, it will be valuable to provide an outline of the evolution of the main styles of the time, together with some account of the major architects and of the development of building techniques and materials.

Morris and Ruskin

While the High Gothic Revival and the loose Victorian forms of Classicism were both flourishing in 1860, the Arts and Crafts movement was born through the work of some of those Gothic architects and their craftsmen. The movement's most famous cradle was the firm of Morris and Company, which expanded in a small village near London. William Morris (1834–96), the architect Philip Webb (1831–1915) and their friends had been fired by the call for higher standards of craftsmanship and the rejection of machine-made materials and decoration in *The Stones of Venice*, the book by the art critic, historian and theorist John Ruskin, published in the year of the Great Exhibition. Morris and Co. designed and produced innumerable furnishings and household objects of many kinds during the following years, while Webb (apart from his designs of various items for the firm) built a series of houses using vernacular building manners and materials drawn from their localities, rather than a particular historical 'artistic' style. The contribution of Morris, however, has often been exaggerated at the expense of designers and Gothic architects such as G. E. Street (1824–81) and G. F. Bodley (1827–1907), who worked with similar ideals in their great practices.

'Queen Anne' and Eclecticism

Webb's approach was not widely taken up until the 1880s, but in the meantime Norman Shaw (1831–1912), the most talented and influential English architect of the

Fig. 6 The manufacture of architectural decoration.
Carton-pierre ornament workshop, George Jackson and Sons Ltd, 49 Rathbone Place, London in 1908.

late nineteenth century, took up the style developed by some of his contemporaries in about 1870 and widely known as the Queen Anne style. The aim was a new 'sweetness and light'[1] in house design, and the style was a mixture of Dutch and even Gothic features with the typical English domestic manner of around 1700. It rejected purism of historical styles and by 1890 this process had sired numerous buildings in Britain of all sizes which used an eclectic mixture of features drawn from many different sources.

As with almost any other architectural style, the eclectic approach could produce designs of great splendour and discipline, or others which were little more than a

Fig. 7   Late Victorian Eclectic architecture. New Scotland Yard (police headquarters), Victoria Embankment, Westminster (1887–90) by Norman Shaw. The design incorporates elements of the Baroque and Scottish Baronial in a strong free architectural style of its own.

jumble of spare parts. Sir Thomas Jackson (1835–1924) used it with great distinction in many of his buildings at Oxford, as did Sir Ernest George (1839–1922) and Thomas Collcutt (1840–1924) in their London buildings such as George's Albemarle Hotel and Collcutt's Imperial Institute of the early 1890s. The biggest and boldest of the eclectic architects of the time was the Mancunian, Alfred Waterhouse (1830–1905), who had a different approach to style. Basically a Gothic architect, Waterhouse said forthrightly that he adopted a style to suit the function of a building, and he only chose it after he had worked out the plan and the structure of the design. Thus, Waterhouse's remaining big London works, which include the Natural History Museum and University College Hospital as well as the famous Prudential Assurance building, vary stylistically as much from each other as they do from their remote historical precedents. The men just mentioned were very much artist-architects (Waterhouse was a Royal Academician), but varieties of eclecticism can be seen in the work of the successful commercial firms of the time, such as Archer and Green of the Hyde Park Hotel and Colonel Edis of Grand Buildings in Trafalgar Square.

Arts and Crafts

While all these exuberant combinations were going on, a number of younger men were following and developing the Arts and Crafts approach of Ruskin, Morris and Webb. The result was the foundation of a number of guilds and societies in the 1880s to discuss and demonstrate ways in which the artistic standards of contemporary architecture and decorative art could be improved. The guilds included architects, sculptors, painters, designers and varied craftsmen among their members. The first was the short-lived Century Guild, founded in 1883 by the architect Arthur Mackmurdo (1851–1942).

In the following year, five young architects, who worked or had worked for Norman Shaw, founded the Art Workers' Guild, which still operates today. The five founders, all important in their various ways, were William Lethaby (1857–1931), Edward Prior (1852–1932), Ernest Newton (1856–1922), Mervyn Macartney (1853–1932) and Gerald Horsley (1862–1917). Among those who joined the Guild in the early years were other talented architects such as Henry Wilson (1863–1934), C. F. A. Voysey (1857–1941), Ernest Gimson (1864–1920), James MacLaren (1843–90, who died young after doing some influential works) and Halsey Ricardo (1854–1928). These were the core of the group of architects who were to bring about what became known as the English Domestic Revival of the 1890s. Their works and evolving style were displayed by the Arts and Crafts Exhibition Society founded in 1889, and their leading theorist was Lethaby. The other central figures who must be mentioned at this point were Charles Robert Ashbee (1863–1942), who followed another of Ruskin's ideas by starting the Guild of Handicraft with local workmen in 1888 in the East End of London, and M. H. Baillie Scott (1865–1945), whose talents emerged rather later in the capital.

For, in London itself, it was Voysey and Ashbee who built the best known early Arts and Crafts houses (see chapter four) of the 1890s, while their fellows often obtained commissions from art-loving middle-class people for the smallish country houses which are such a feature of the period. The products of Voysey's simplified white roughcast style were widely illustrated in the architects' and builders'

Fig. 8 Arts and Crafts architecture. Studio Cottage, 14 South Parade, Bedford Park, London (1891). Simplified forms and white walls were the keynote of Voysey's type of Arts and Crafts design at this time, widely influential among the builders of suburban villas in many parts of England.

magazines and it was his manner that was most frequently adopted by contractor–developers when the major growth of the outer suburbs of London started soon after 1900. The crowded interiors of the Victorian home started to give way to a lighter, more airy type with inventive detailing of the sort practised by George Walton (1867–1933), Charles Rennie Mackintosh's friend who moved from Glasgow to London in 1898, and by the fathers of English town planning, Raymond Unwin (1863–1940) and Barry Parker (1867–1947) in their Hampstead Garden Suburb of 1906 onwards, where Baillie Scott and others built Arts and Crafts houses.

The Arts and Crafts movement itself was subject to changes in its objectives and stylistic fashions over the years.[2] By 1906, many of its leading architects had at last realised that the classically-based domestic style of the early eighteenth century was as valid a vernacular English manner, especially in towns, as the other local styles which they had adopted in different parts of the country. It was therefore not to be dismissed as a foreign importation just because it had features of Classicism. From that time onwards, more and more of these architects, without sacrificing Arts and Crafts standards, moved into the practice of a freely inventive Neo-Georgian style which flourished for thirty or forty years.

Art Nouveau or Arts and Crafts?

Although the term is used, as a generality there was no Art Nouveau architecture in England. The continental Art Nouveau buildings were descended structurally from various sources, including Viollet le Duc's experiments, while adopting and developing the curvilinear decorative style which had some origins in William Morris's furnishing designs. The term Art Nouveau has become a popular catchword to describe the freely inventive manner of the Arts and Crafts movement around 1900, but the links between the two were superficial in the extreme. Arts and Crafts designers of talent and integrity insisted that valid originality could only be derived from natural forms growing from roots deep in the native past of their own country, and building forms which were suited to their materials and their functions. These ideas were a direct continuation of those of Augustus Welby Pugin, the founding ideologist of Victorian Gothic architecture and in this respect the Arts and Crafts movement must be seen as the direct outcome of the Gothic revival.

English Free Style

Thus the inventive brilliance that can be seen in the London office buildings (see chapter seven) of Treadwell and Martin (Henry Treadwell 1861–1910 and Leonard Martin 1869–1935) is developed from the Gothic style, with other ingredients thrown in and the stirring done with a spoon of originality. Similarly small business premises by that wayward genius Beresford Pite (1861–1934) are derived from a different strand of Arts and Crafts thought – the desire to combine sculpture of artistic quality with architectural detailing.

The most notable appearance of highly decorated Arts and Crafts architecture in the years just before 1900 was in the work of Henry Wilson, a central figure in the movement who (with T. Phillips Figgis) built the influential library in Ladbroke

Grove as early as 1891, and of Charles Harrison Townsend (1851–1928). Townsend's buildings – such as the Bishopsgate Institute, the Horniman Museum and the Whitechapel Art Gallery – are undoubtedly the most impressive large works of the Arts and Crafts Free Style before economic and other influences brought simplicity and discipline to this anti-copyist approach in the early 1900s. Viewing the wilder elements in Townsend's decorative detailing, it is not surprising to learn that many of his clients were charitable bodies who felt vaguely that a new style was suitable for their edifices, rather than business or government clients who looked for tradition and grandeur. Nor is it astonishing to learn that, although Townsend was a devoted and well-liked member of the Art Workers' Guild, he was not one of the inner circle of the movement who gathered around Lethaby and promoted a more austere taste.

Such decorative links as Arts and Crafts decoration had with Art Nouveau were stamped out shortly after 1900 by a vigorous campaign by leaders of the English movement.[3] The simpler style which replaced it for a few years, before the movement took up a free Neo-Georgian as the true vernacular, had been launched in 1895–98 by A. Dunbar Smith (1866–1933) and Cecil Brewer (1871–1918) in their charitable building, now called Mary Ward House, in Tavistock Place, Bloomsbury. This type of design, soon embraced by the young architects working under Owen Fleming for the London County Council, combined brick with areas of white plaster (see chapter three). Then, in 1900, the young Charles Holden (1875–1960) published his first designs under the name of Percy Adams, his employer, and Holden's sheer power and three-dimensional clarity of design were to provide the culmination of the Free Style in London buildings. Second only to Lutyens during the early decades of the new century, Holden was another designer of great originality with an Arts and Crafts background (he had worked with Ashbee for a year) who gradually integrated the British Georgian tradition in the detailing of his buildings without loss of originality (see chapters seven and fifteen).

The Big Competitions

Another class of Edwardian architects, without Arts and Crafts connections and able to design with brilliance in whatever style suited their commissions, was that of the big competition winners.[4] As far as London was concerned, the leading examples were Henry Hare (1860–1921) and James Gibson (1861–1951). Hare specialised in public libraries and town halls, and his many London libraries show him moving from a distinguished if eclectic free manner to a strong Classicism with English roots. Gibson showed less consistency in his development, with his West Ham Technical College, his Middlesex Guildhall in Parliament Square and his Debenham and Freebody department store in quite different manners. Yet when we come to examine these designs in the relevant chapters, it will be seen that there are understandable reasons for their various styles.

Gothic Church Architecture

A group of architects rather apart from the rest were the specialists in church design, though all of them did some secular work as well. In this type of building, the Gothic

Fig. 9   Late Victorian Gothic architecture. A late design by J. D. Sedding with Henry Wilson. Interior, Holy Trinity Church, Sloane Street, Chelsea (1888–90, furnished by Wilson and others during the eighteen-nineties). The masterpiece of Arts and Crafts Gothic churches in inner London.

style still ruled, symbolising the unaltering attitudes of the Christian hierarchies at a time when the long decline in church congregations had begun (see chapter twelve). Yet the Gothic style itself was altering. The great William Butterfield died in 1900, but G. F. Bodley (1827–1907) was showing in his last London church, Holy Trinity near the Royal Albert Hall, that the style could take on a new light elegance without losing its pure essence.

Other architects followed the Arts and Crafts enthusiast John Dando Sedding (1838–91) into the more mixed forms of Gothicism seen in his famous Holy Trinity Church of 1888–1900 in Sloane Street, Chelsea, completed by his assistant and successor Henry Wilson. The leading designers of Gothic Churches in the years around 1900 included Temple Moore (1856–1920), W. D. Caroe (1857–1938), Basil Champneys (1842–1935), Sir Ninian Comper (1864–1960), Sir Walter Tapper (1861–1935), Sir Charles Nicholson (1867–1949) and the designer of Liverpool Cathedral, Sir Giles Gilbert Scott (1880–1960). The Arts and Crafts influence, together with that of the last churches by Norman Shaw, tended towards a new style developed from late English Perpendicular, with wide pointed arches and wide windows which had fresh forms of stone tracery within them. Such a style can be seen in many of the churches built in the Edwardian decade in the new suburbs, for Anglicans, Methodists, Baptists and other sects.

The Byzantine Churches

The other popular style for churches of this period was the free Byzantine. Byzantine architecture was studied and practised by Arts and Crafts architects in the early 1890s, but it was brought to many people's attention by the great Roman Catholic Cathedral of Westminster, built by the architect John Francis Bentley (1839–1902) at the turn of the century. The Byzantine style was very often used in Roman Catholic churches in many parts of England from that time onwards, perhaps symbolising the Catholic claim to be rooted in the early days of Christianity and its architecture. But in London, as will be seen in chapter twelve, there are also several examples of its use in Anglican churches before the outbreak of the Great War. Bentley's cathedral is in fact a very eclectic building, with various fashionable motifs of the 1890s successfully blended with the overall Byzantine manner.

The English Baroque

Many other architects of large buildings were starting to react against total eclecticism by the late 1890s and to look for a new approach to a national style fit for the Empire's capital. As early as 1889, John Brydon (1840–1901), architect of the recently completed Chelsea Vestry Hall, was lecturing to the London Architectural Association on 'The English Renaissance', saying that the style of late Wren and

Fig. 10 The Baroque revival.
Entrance front, Institute of Chartered Accountants, Moorgate Place, City of London (1888–93) by John Belcher and A. Beresford Pite. The design influenced many architects, showing that the Baroque was a suitable style for realising Arts and Crafts ideals of fine sculpture and painting as part of architecture.

Vanbrugh was by 1720 'fairly established as the national style – the vernacular of the country'.[5] This attitude to the style, which later came to be called English Baroque, made a tremendous difference to a generation of architects engulfed by the impure splendours of eclecticism and obsessed with the idea of forming a new style 'which is to become the style of the future',[6] for the country at the centre of a great empire. For if the Baroque of about 1720 was a truly English style, rather than just an import from abroad, then it offered the solution to these architects' problem.

Moreover, the Baroque style did not inhibit originality – for it did not follow the rules of proportion and strict logic of Renaissance Classicism – and it even supplied a suitable backdrop for the original aim of the Art Workers' Guild, to bring together the arts of fine architecture, fine sculpture and fine painting in buildings where some display was suitable.

The first notable building in the new 'artistic' Baroque manner was the Institute of Chartered Accountants in the City of London, opened in 1893 and designed by John Belcher (1841–1913) and his assistant Beresford Pite (1861–1934). Later, the Arts and Crafts element became submerged, though much of the sculpture was excellent. By 1897, the year of Queen Victoria's Diamond Jubilee, the style was all the rage and countless town halls, government buildings and imposing office blocks were designed and built in this 'English Renaissance' or Edwardian Baroque manner during the following nine years and even later. The great names of this Baroque period, apart from those already mentioned such as Belcher and Brydon, were Sir A. Brumwell Thomas (1868–1948), Sir Aston Webb (1849–1930), Lanchester and Rickards (H. V. Lanchester 1863–1953 and E. A. Rickards 1872–1920) and Edward Mountford (1855–1908). In the second rank, mention should be made of William Young (1843–1900), the theatre architect Frank Matcham (1854–1920), Sir William Emerson (1843–1924), R. Frank Atkinson (1869–1923), Dunn and Watson (William Dunn, 1859–1934, and Robert Watson, d. 1916, in partnership with W. Curtis Green, 1875–1960) and A. Marshall Mackenzie and Son. Like other older architects, Sir Aston Webb came to the Baroque style from a background of eclectic design, and he developed the largest practice of his time culminating in the Admiralty Arch and the new front of Buckingham Palace. The most distinguished of these older men to take up the manner were Sir Ernest George (1839–1922) and Norman Shaw himself, whose Gaiety Theatre and Piccadilly Hotel were among its best London products. But mention of the other big works in London must await their respective chapters, for many of the most splendid buildings of Westminster and the West End are Edwardian Baroque (see chapter seventeen).

Among the quieter specimens of the office buildings of the Baroque period were the new premises for *Country Life* magazine, dating from 1903. This work was most notable for launching the London career of the greatest British architect of the early twentieth century, Sir Edwin Lutyens (1869–1944). Lutyens came from an Arts and Crafts domestic practice in Surrey which produced some of the very finest country houses of the 1890s. His early London buildings should be particularly noticed, since they pointed the way towards the charming and inventive Neo-Georgian style which was to be the truly English path of the Arts and Crafts movement, after its Free Style period up to about 1900, and after the extravagances of the Baroque started to die down following the building depression of 1906. Other architects who played leading roles in this transition, even earlier than Lutyens, were Ernest Newton (1856–1922), Leonard Stokes (1858–1925), Sir Frank Elgood (1865–1948), Macartney and of course Holden. But first there was a French Neo-Classical interlude in London in the second half of King Edward's reign.

French Classicism

With the exception of some short periods, Frenchness had denoted social smartness in London since the eighteenth century. Various French-influenced versions of the Classical style had long been popular in England for apartments for the wealthy and for restaurants and theatres. Indeed, the extraordinary number of London theatres built around 1900 (see chapter nine) were more often French in feeling than English. Matcham used a transformed version of the English Baroque for the Coliseum, but most of his other works tasted of France in one way or another. His two successful pupils in practice at the end of the century were Bertie Crewe (d. 1936) and the highly distinguished W. G. R. Sprague (c.1865–1933). Sprague, who designed a phenomenal number of the best-loved theatres in London today, was intensely Francophile. His Wyndham's Theatre of 1899 will serve as an early instance of the French taste which was to follow in his other work of the Edwardian era.

It was King Edward himself who turned Francophilia into a widespread fashion with his famous Paris visit of 1903. Before that, relations between France and England had been hostile for many decades. The Paris crowds booed when the King arrived, but were cheering by the time he left three days later after some enthusiastic speeches about France. The politicians took over and the Entente Cordiale followed. Among architects, the Paris Exhibition of 1900 had made a vivid impression – both in its Art Nouveau decorative work, which made the English shudder, and in the grandeur of the Beaux Arts Classical buildings. It was precisely in the year of the King's visit that a major French Classical building started to go up in London. This was the Ritz Hotel in Piccadilly, designed by the Parisian Charles Mewès (1860–1914) and his young English partner Arthur J. Davis (1878–1951), who had been trained at the Ecole des Beaux-Arts. Mewès and Davis followed the Ritz with other notable buildings in the West End, and the French influence found much favour among those who called for a purer and simpler Classicism when taste turned against the Baroque in 1906. The leading spokesman in this campaign was Sir Reginald Blomfield (1856–1942), who had moved from involvement with the Arts and Crafts movement to become an exponent of French Classicism, partly as a result of writing a monumental book on the history of French architecture.[7] Blomfield's Royal Academy lectures of 1907 and his buildings, such as the United University Club of 1906–07, contributed much to the new French fashion.

Other architects notable at this Francophile stage included Frank Verity (1864–1937, see chapter five on Mansion Blocks), Sir Albert Richardson (1880–1964), Fernand Billerey (the French partner of Detmar Blow), and the great Scottish architect Sir John Burnet (1857–1938). Burnet designed the Neo-Classical King Edward VII Galleries of the British Museum in 1904 and thereafter moved much of his practice from Glasgow to London. Among his many remarkable works of the next few years, he was appointed executive architect of the later stages of the huge Selfridge's Department Store in Oxford Street, which first brought American Neo-Classical design to London.

Fig. 11 (*Following page*)   The English Neo-Georgian style.
No. 28 South Street, Mayfair (1902) by Detmar Blow. By the early 1900s, many Arts and Crafts architects, such as Blow, had accepted that the Georgian style offered the most valid vernacular manner for London.

Reinforced Concrete

Reinforced concrete frames were close behind steel. By 1901, Arts and Crafts architects were already experimenting with mass concrete structure and with concrete floors in buildings outside London. An office building with reinforced concrete roofs in the outskirts of Manchester followed in 1906, and the reinforced concrete framed Liver Building at Liverpool in 1908. In the capital, reinforced concrete made slower progress. According to Andrew Saint, the earliest example is probably A. C. Blomfield's Friars House, in Broad Street, City (1906–08). The technical architectural books of the period recommended the new material cautiously. 'Although concrete cannot be disposed quite so advantageously as can steel ... yet the conjunction of concrete and steel is found, in the majority of cases to which it is applicable, to be cheaper than metal alone, even for bridging spans as large as 150 feet', wrote P. R. Strong in 1907 in one such book.[9] Strong particularly recommended its value for floors but was less enthusiastic about its use in frame structure. This was partly due to the limited experience in calculation at the time. 'It is impossible to arrive at any very definite figures on which to base calculations, while at the same time the disposition of stresses in beams, etc. has by no means been accurately established.' So, in general, concrete frame structure was used in fairly small buildings in London before the Great War of 1914–18, of which Norman Shaw's very last building (see chapter eighteen) is a surprising example. As late as 1913, William Lethaby, the Arts and Crafts evangelist for an architecture based on structure, was telling the Architectural Association,[10] 'It must be admitted that, notwithstanding its virtues, concrete has certain special defects ... Big rounded forms seem suggested by this plastic material'.

Brick and Stone

Among other building materials, both brick and stone underwent something of a renaissance in 1900. The Arts and Crafts movement had called for and brought about improved standards in the craft of fine brickmaking – with handmade bricks enjoying a revival for a time – and bricklaying, which had notable results in the detailed quality of many buildings in the 1900s. At the same time, the demand for stone for the new public and prestige buildings caused a renewal of activity in the famous quarries of Portland and to some extent, Bath.

Terracotta and Glazed Bricks

Terracotta, too, that favourite baked clay decorative material of the Victorians, continued to be used on a gradually diminishing scale in the 1900s. But the building materials most particularly associated with Edwardian London are the coloured or white glazed bricks and glazed tiles for which the Arts and Crafts architect Halsey Ricardo had long campaigned. Glazed tiles, notably those designed by William de Morgan and Ricardo himself, had long been popular inside houses. In their simple white form, glazed bricks had self-cleaning properties which made them popular for the rear façades of buildings whose street frontages seemed to their clients to call for

prestigious stone. But Ricardo urged their use on the front elevations too. Not only would they save cleaning costs in the grimy London atmosphere, he claimed in lecture after lecture, but they would provide a reflected light and bright colour which would bring gladness to the hearts of Londoners emerging from the gloom of the new underground railway.[11] Apart from Ricardo's own gleaming green and blue mansion for the department store millionaire Debenham in Addison Road (see chapter five), the underground stations themselves, Debenham's big department store in Wigmore Street and a number of other London buildings used these shining materials to cover their outer walls.

Fig. 13   Edwardian glazed tiles.
Debenham and Freebody's Department Store, Wigmore Street, Marylebone (1906–08) by James Gibson. The walls are of glazed Doulton tiles and this photograph shows the steel frame of the high dome before cladding.

3 Housing for the Working Class

Writing in 1901, a commentator on London noted,

The overcrowding of the Metropolis is perhaps the most pressing social problem of the day, and the most difficult to cope with. The poorer classes must live near their place of employment, being unable to afford even the smallest and cheapest railway-fare; while the value of land anywhere near the centres of business is so great, and the demolition of small houses thereon to make room for big warehouses so continuous, that the filthiest and most meagre lodgings are filled to overflowing, though let for rents that absorb nearly all the scanty earnings of the tenants, The average rent paid for a one-room tenement in some parts is 3s. 10¾d. a week, while in Spitalfield it is between 4s. 6d. and 6s.[1]

What did such a scale of rents, about one-fifth of £1 or more per week for a single room, mean to poor people? A clerk could not afford to marry at that time until he earned £90 a year,[2] but he would then expect to rent a small house at about 8s. a week or about £21 a year. For the really poor in central London the picture was very different. The rent of about £11 a year would have to come out of a workman's income of perhaps £30 or out of an unsupported woman's of sometimes only £13 a year.

Amongst women, the most hardly-earned wages are those of tailoresses (at 5s. 3d. per week working 9 a.m. to 9 p.m. including Sundays). The wages of the shirt-maker are even more shameful ... if she could by any possibility do two dozen a day, her wages would not exceed 3s. 6d. a week. Other occupations for women–somewhat better paid–are the shelling of walnuts or peas ... fur-pulling and the preparation of animal entrails for manufacture into sausage skins.[3]

The result of this situation was the multiple sharing of rooms, overcrowded lodging houses and pockets of central London with high rates of malnutrition, disease and crime. A later commentator, who had known London in 1900, imagined a visitor in 1934 who had not seen the city for a third of a century.[4] 'An early impression would be the absence of abject and paraded poverty ... he would remember that in his day (1900) one saw barefooted children in utter rags, and workless men with knees showing through their torn trousers, eating refuse from dustbins.' The achievement of making such sights into rarities belongs to the first third of the twentieth century, although destitute people can still be seen occasionally today.

Concern about the housing of the poor was not new even in 1900. A reformer and publicist, M. Kaufman, pointed this out[5] in 1907. 'This subject has now been occupying public attention for two generations. It was in 1842 that the late Lord Shaftesbury took it up ... However, it is only of late that it has reached the dignity of a national movement ... It is in the inner belt, between the city and the suburbs, where the evils of overcrowding are most acutely felt ... thirty-one people were found to

Fig. 14   Family in a slum dwelling, 1901.

occupy one small room in central London. But the last census revealed the fact that at least 3000 Londoners live eight or more in a room, that over 9000 live seven or more in a room and about 26 000 of whom six or more live in one room.' Kaufman goes on to tell of the experiments in re-housing the working classes during the late nineteenth century; the new housing blocks in London built by the Peabody Donation Fund since 1862 and, by then, providing over 11 000 hygienic living rooms; Octavia Hill's purchase from 1884 onwards of overcrowded houses in London slums and re-allocation of the tenants while educating them in clean habits (she ended up with 5000 houses under her management); the model villages built by philanthropic industrialists such as George Cadbury at Bourneville near Birmingham and W. H. Lever at Port Sunlight near Liverpool. But Kaufman saw that these experiments were only trailblazers. By 1890 the doctrine of Collectivism was widely enough accepted by politicians for a start to be made on the long slow process of action on a large scale by local government authorities.

In London, this meant action by the London County Council, formed in 1889 following the *County Councils Act* of 1888. An Architect's Department was formed in 1890 as a reincarnation of the Metropolitan Board of Works, with Thomas Blashill as Architect to the Council and the young Owen Fleming as Head Architect of the

Fig. 15   The Boundary Street area, a slum known as 'The Jago', Shoreditch, before demolition in 1897.

Housing Division. They were very different characters. Blashill was continuing his previous steady service as architect to the M.B.W. while Fleming had been a prominent student at the Architectural Association in London, with ardent Socialist convictions confirmed by his contact with William Morris, Philip Webb and Lethaby. It was partly Fleming's vigour, with that of the team gathered in the Housing Division and the managerial skill of the experienced Blashill, which got the L.C.C.'s housing programme gradually under way despite the inevitable delays in political decision-making by the Council and central government.

The L.C.C.'s policy was one of demolition of the most virulent plague-spots and slums, followed by the construction of new housing blocks on the site, well separated by open yards and occasional garden areas.

Progress was slow at first, for the machinery of local government decision, demolition, roadworks and rebuilding often took a decade. The *Housing of the Working Classes Act* of 1890 gave the L.C.C. the duty and power to make compulsory purchases and demolish unfit properties. Plans were immediately made to re-develop a notorious slum called The Jago around Boundary Street, Shoreditch, in the East End. But the administrative procedure, including alterations required by the Secretary of State, prevented work from starting until 1897.

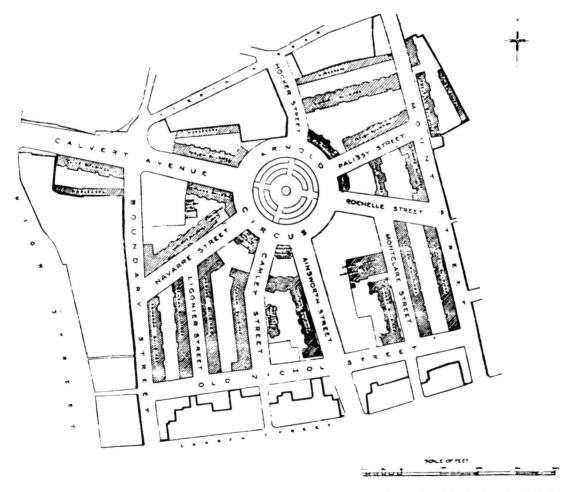

Fig. 16 The Boundary Street area as rebuilt with new streets and housing blocks by the L.C.C. Architect's Department in 1897–1900.

The external architectural qualities of the estate were to some extent Fleming's responsibility. Following Blashill's paper on dwellings in blocks, given to the Architectural Association in February 1900, Fleming said in the discussion reported in *The Builder* magazine that he was sure the older man was wrong to say that the exteriors were unimportant; Fleming felt that working class people were affected by ugly or attractive buildings as much as the other classes. The L.C.C. architects altered the old grid pattern of the streets completely, producing a street plan which radiates from a central garden, with five-storey housing blocks designed by several individual architects on the Housing Division's staff. The blocks around this central garden are harsh on their street frontages, but the internal courtyards of each show a fascinating originality of form and detail, with high white upper storeys and gables contrasting with the brickwork. The southern blocks were designed by Charles Winmill.

The Boundary Street estate was only completed, and opened by the Prince of Wales, in March 1900, registering the first of many major developments by the L.C.C. It was in 1899 that Blashill retired as Architect to the L.C.C. He was succeeded by W. E. Riley, an energetic building manager, who collected much of the credit for

Fig. 17   Internal courtyard of Clifton Buildings housing block, in the Boundary Street housing estate, Shoreditch (1897–1900) by the L.C.C. Architect's Department. Designed by Charles Winmill.
Fig. 18   Housing block in Herrick Street, Westminster, on the L.C.C.'s Millbank Estate (1897–1902). The space in each apartment and the wide tree-lined streets between the blocks were exceptional for the time.

projects reaching completion after many years, but did indeed hasten the pace of the work.

The Millbank Estate behind the Tate Gallery, built in 1897–1903 on part of the site of the recently demolished Millbank Prison, attracted even more attention at the time than had Boundary Street. Again, it consists of five-storey housing blocks in well-treed and fairly wide streets, with a central public garden. The originality of design is only slightly less remarkable here than at Boundary Street – it is a little more severe and less fanciful. Millbank is only one of many such L.C.C. estates built during these years.[6] During the first eight years of the century, twelve major estates of housing blocks opened in inner London, providing new flats of a reasonable standard for over 17 000 people.

The architectural style adopted for this housing by the L.C.C. Architect's Department was very particular, though unobtrusive, and the pre-1914 blocks are as immediately recognisable in many parts of London as are the London Board Schools of the 1870s. The style is derived partly from a magnification of the simple Georgian vernacular London house, partly from the domestic works of Philip Webb and Norman Shaw (and perhaps C. R. Ashbee), and partly from the results of visits by

Fig. 19 Bruce House (hostel for single working men), Drury Lane, Covent Garden (1905–07) by the L.C.C. Architect's Department.

Fleming and his colleagues to public housing in Vienna and elsewhere. The aim was very much 'sweetness and light', a simplified version of the 'Queen Anne' style with its combination of good brickwork and the white-painted woodwork of tall windows. The walls are high and unadorned, with steeply pitched roofs above, but the detailing of doorways and treatment of corners often shows much ingenuity. The buildings can provide a fairly depressing environment on dull winter days with no leaves on the trees, but with sunshine and summer greenery one can still see what a brave new standard they set in 1900 for slum-dwellers.

Apart from housing for families, the L.C.C. aimed to provide suitable lodgings for single men and women too, especially for the single working-class man. One of these, Bruce House in Kemble Street, Covent Garden, opened in 1907, a brickwork cliff of six storeys with interesting detailing at ground level and hipped gables at the top. It does not achieve any sort of domestic friendliness, but it is still used for its original purpose. Typical charges for this and the other hostels at Deptford, Camden Town and at Elephant and Castle in the early 1900s were 7d. a night or 3s. 6d. for a week.

The large redevelopments and housing blocks were not without their critics at the time.

Evil is intensified by the efforts of sanitary reforms in demolishing condemned dwellings and whole areas of houses and, in so doing, turning out thousands into the streets ... they are driven into the slums, overcrowded already, and forced to create new slums ... These huge erections, some five or six, or even seven storeys high ... are called 'sky-scrapers' ...

Fig. 20   Cottages on the L.C.C.'s Totterdown Fields Estate, Tooting (1903–11). The first of the Council's large developments to provide individual suburban houses, rather than flats in housing blocks which replaced Central London slums.

Packed and piled up, storey upon storey, these people can scarcely enjoy the ordinary comfort and decencies of home life,

wrote Kaufman.[7] What he proposed instead were 'cottages cheap not nasty' in the outer suburbs, ideally with places of work near them.

The L.C.C. was in fact ahead of Kaufman. The *Housing of the Working Classes Act* of 1900 empowered local authorities to purchase land outside their own boundaries and build houses on it. The L.C.C. quickly bought a large tract of land in South London at Tooting and between 1903 and 1911 built 1229 cottages to house 8788 people. The cottages on this Totterdown Fields Estate[8] off Church Lane, Tooting, are simple and attractive, in brick and white plaster with some striking gables and individualistic detailing, although the streets are in an unimaginative grid pattern. Rents for a three-room house were 6s. 6d. a week, for a five-room house 13s. 6d. Some of the houses had baths.

The other major L.C.C. cottage estate of this period is more imaginatively arranged. This is in North London, the White Hart Lane Estate[9] in Tottenham. Due to various delays, work was not started in Tottenham until 1911. By 1912, 781 cottages had been built between Lordship Lane and Risley Avenue, a small part of the forty-eight acre area. Again, the houses are simple and pleasant (though less original than at Totterdown), with wider streets and a varied lay-out. There is a public garden within one quadrangle of houses and other green patches. The cost of these first-stage dwellings was £175 for a three-room house, £245 for those with five rooms. Electric

Fig. 21   Cottages on the L.C.C.'s Totterdown Fields Estate (1903–11).

tramways were built, rather tardily, to connect the Tooting and Tottenham estates with central London.

Work continued on the White Hart Lane Estate and others such as Old Oak, for many years. Indeed the L.C.C. Architect's Department was only at the start of its long history of providing new and better housing for poorer Londoners. It is hard to judge the Department's success or failure during the Edwardian period, for opinions have always differed sharply. For example, one writer wrote in 1934 of the inner London housing blocks,

> Apart from being a good deal uglier than the original slums, they did nothing to solve the problem … They merely replaced overcrowded alleys with overcrowded boxes. They took away the lateral slums and created a series of vertical slums … The later development of Council estates on the outskirts was a much more sensible idea and … will no doubt in time, by combining with the satellite towns and industries, prove to be the solution to the problem.[10]

In view of subsequent experience with housing policy and its results, we may well agree with only part of this view and may be less critical of the L.C.C.'s early efforts. Architecturally, and socially, they are far from being the worst L.C.C. housing of the twentieth century, while the sheer organisation and patience needed to get them built constitutes a considerable achievement.

4 The House and the Suburb

By the early twentieth century the achievements of British architects and designers in creating new standards of beauty and simplicity for houses and their furnishings were widely acclaimed. A leading London architectural magazine, *The Builder*, commented in May 1900 on the annual exhibition of the Home Arts and Industries Association,[1] noting 'the revival of the old English handicrafts. For several decades these have been obliterated by the use of machinery and their revival is due to the teaching of Ruskin and Morris, and to this Association.' In fact, the Arts and Crafts Exhibition Society was just as influential. The German government sent the architect Hermann Muthesius to London in the late 1890s as a Cultural Attaché to their embassy to study the revival in English architecture, and Muthesius's resulting books, including *Das Englische Haus* (Berlin: 1904–05), increased the already high reputation of Arts and Crafts architecture throughout northern Europe. In 1903 Mr M. Folcka, the Swedish representative on the jury at the Turin International Exhibition, paid tribute[2] to the English Arts and Crafts movement.

> You all know where we have to look for the origin of this movement of which we see around us at this exhibition the actual results; ... with which are inseparably joined the names of William Morris, of Edward Burne-Jones and Walter Crane ... I take the liberty to propose that we create a grand and unique Diploma of Special Honour as an act of homage and thankfulness to England.

This movement, which became known as the English Domestic Revival, coincided with developing ideas about garden cities and in London with the start of the major spread of the suburbs around London which will be examined in this chapter. Between 1900 and 1914 the built-up area of London almost doubled, and most of that growth was in residential suburbs beyond a circle of eight miles radius from Charing Cross. A few of those thousands of houses were designed by the architects who had taken up and established the Arts and Crafts domestic movement from 1890 onwards. More of them were the work of talented younger architects inspired by the charm and originality of the new approach. But the great majority of these terraced, semi-detached and detached suburban houses built after 1900 were the work of obscure local architects or of the builder-developers' own draughtsmen, working from the designs by famous names illustrated in many building magazines and books.[3] Thus it is easy to go around Edwardian suburbs such as Golders Green and Hendon in the north or Barnes, Morden and Mitcham in the south and to notice the derivations of the frontages of many houses.

The usual middle class Victorian living room or bedroom was densely decorated and crowded with bulky and curvaceously carved furniture. The move towards more space and simplicity developed gradually. Designs of the 1860s by the architect Philip

Fig. 22 An evening at home with the family around the piano, *c.*1900.

Fig. 23   The crowded decoration and furnishing typical of the years around 1900. Mr J. C. Moreton Thompson's new drawing room at No. 56 Hans Place, Knightsbridge in 1898. The simplifying influence of the Arts and Crafts movement had nothing to offer those who wanted displays of luxury.
Fig. 24   Dining room (*c.*1900) by C. F. A. Voysey.

Webb and his friend, the great designer William Morris, are still cluttered. Simplicity and space – with a touch of Japanese influence – were the keynotes in many of the studio houses designed for the artists of the Aesthetic Movement in Tite Street, Chelsea, by Edward Godwin in the late 1870s. Godwin was the original architect to the first Garden Suburb, Bedford Park in west London, but he was soon replaced by Norman Shaw as it grew from 1877 onwards, a model of smallish houses in green gardens for later middle-class suburbs. Shaw was the most influential domestic architect of the 1880s and many of the Arts and Crafts leaders of the 1890s started their working lives in his office.

The most significant London house designers of that decade, however, moved away from Shaw's manner to one of simpler lines and less decoration. As far as inner London itself was concerned, the leading exponents of domestic lightness in the 1890s were C. F. A. Voysey (1857–1941), C. R. Ashbee (1863–1942) and their followers.

Two of Voysey's earliest houses are in London, both built in 1891. The first design, the studio cottage at No. 14 South Parade in Bedford Park, challenges its red brick neighbours by its white roughcast walls and band stone-dressed windows. The forms are simple but are given delicacy by the rooflines and the slender brackets supporting the gutters. At Bedford Park, Voysey built up to three storeys to give the accommodation needed on a small site. His other studio house of the same year, at No. 17 St Dunstan's Road in West Kensington, spreads back into its garden on two storeys and is far more typical of the classic Voysey suburban or country house with its banded windows emphasising the horizontal lines. The tall iron railings in front of this house show the simple elegance of much good Arts and Crafts metalwork.

Although he was not a propagandist to compare with his Arts and Crafts contemporary William Lethaby, Voysey spoke on many occasions to spread his ideas among his fellow architects. In 1892 he told the Architectural Association in London,[4] 'The fact is that we are overdecorated ... Begin by casting out all the useless ornaments and remove the dust-catching flounces and furbelows ... Eschew all imitations. Strive to produce an effect of repose and simplicity'. Wherever possible, he would persuade his clients to let him design the furnishings of his houses, down to the table silver.

During the following decade, apart from many extensions and internal redecorations, Voysey designed and built several more houses in London and its suburbs. Most of them were illustrated in architectural magazines and his influence can be seen in the work of many other architects from 1895 onwards.

Voysey's design of 1892 for three houses in Hans Road off Knightsbridge was altered and reduced to Nos. 14 and 15 as built, but it shows the possible application of his lean and elegant lines to an inner London street with no space between the houses. The design is particularly noteworthy as it is one of Voysey's very few truly urban works, in contrast to his more usual anti-urban domestic architecture.

In 1896 Voysey built a house for his father, an eccentric clergyman dismissed from the Church of England for preaching that hell does not exist, at No. 8 Platts Lane in Hampstead. In this design he used ideas which he seems to have developed with his neighbour and friend Edward Prior, an Arts and Crafts extremist whose major works are outside London. Instead of building the house near the street end of the corner plot with a conventional back garden, Voysey designed an L-shaped plan at the back of the site and left the front area free for lawns and trees. Here again are the white-painted roughcast, low horizontal lines, characteristic roofs and high chimney stacks which give his designs their elegance.

The interiors of Voysey's houses showed increasing variety as the years passed.

The spaces are usually long and broad with comparatively low ceilings for their time. The beams often protrude in long lines beneath the ceiling, upright chairs designed by him are dramatically vertical but windows and other features are predominantly horizontal. The decoration is novel for its time but very restrained, often with his favourite motif, a heart. Later, arches and panelling appeared increasingly, perhaps the result of pressure from his clients or perhaps of a widening of his own taste.

Other talented architects were helping to spread the new approach to house design and decoration during the 1890s. Most of them were members of the Art Workers' Guild, where discussion evenings about design and crafts were held regularly, and of the Arts and Crafts Exhibition Society, whose annual displays showed the products of the movement to the public and the building trade. As far as inner London is concerned, the most significant of these architects was Charles Robert Ashbee. Ashbee held radically progressive political views and put them into action. In 1888 he had adapted the current ideas of university settlements in London slumland, which will be described in chapter thirteen, to the arts and the crafts by founding the Guild of Handicraft in the poor East End of London. There, by 1902, fifty local men had been trained as skilled craftsmen, producing furniture and other household objects, usually from Ashbee's own distinguished designs.

Ashbee himself was an architect, a craftwork designer and a prolific author. The

Fig. 25   Studio house, No. 17 St Dunstan's Road, West Kensington (1891) by C. F. A. Voysey.

houses which he designed in inner London were a notable contribution to domestic architecture. They were grouped in Cheyne Walk, Chelsea, and the destruction of all but two of them, by bombs during the second world war or by later demolition, is a sad loss. The first of the series was the house which Ashbee built for himself in 1894 at No. 37 Cheyne Walk, called the Magpie and Stump after the public house which had occupied the site. This house, with its long bow window, was a new development from the 'Queen Anne' style associated with Norman Shaw and others during the 1870–90 period.

The next Ashbee design was very different and very bold. Nos. 72–73, built in 1897, was a double house of a London type produced earlier by E. W. Godwin and by James Maclaren.[5] A half-basement door led to the apartment occupying the lower two storeys on the centre and right-hand side of the house, while the higher front door led to a stairway up to the rooms spread across the top three floors of the house. The materials were absolutely simple brickwork, with sparse touches of decoration, and Ashbee obtained an effect of strange elegance solely by the placing and shapes of the windows and doors.

Both the buildings mentioned above have been destroyed. The two surviving Ashbee houses in Cheyne Walk are Nos. 38 and 39, built in 1899–1901. No. 39 is relatively straightforward, with tall narrow windows so close to each other that they

Fig. 26   First design for Nos. 12, 14 and 16 Hans Road (1892) by C. F. A. Voysey. Only the two left-hand houses were built in 1894 and the design was altered. This is one of the few examples of an urban Voysey design for terrace (as against suburban or rural detached) houses.

Fig. 27   Nos. 38 and 39 Cheyne Walk, Chelsea (1899–1901) by C. R. Ashbee.

almost become horizontal bands. No. 38 is more complex, with a front door below ground level and a delicate arrangement of windows on the upper plastered levels. The most striking feature is the tall gable, chopped off at one side to align with its neighbouring house. Both houses have distinguished iron railings at street level.

The interiors of the houses continue the austere elegance of manner, relieved by some mural paintings of a type which the architect liked. Ashbee had at least his fair share of self-esteem and was often scornful of other architects' work. But it is hard to doubt that Voysey, whose conservative political opinions were antipathetic to progressives, had some influence in forming Ashbee's own very personal manner. Most of the lines in these interiors are straight and the forms are slender. Curves are usually restricted to details and tend to be sinuous in the manner typical of much Arts and Crafts design. In his later Cheyne Walk houses, No. 75 of 1902 and No. 71 of 1912 (both destroyed), Ashbee incorporated touches of Classicism as Arts and Crafts designers came to recognise that Georgian detailing was a part of the old English vernacular and so within their scope for adaptation.

In the inner suburbs of London the nineteenth century left few areas available for new houses, for the cost of land was so high that mansion blocks of flats – which will be described in the next chapter – became popular and economical. Here and there, in desirable positions, there were fields which had not yet been developed. The houses designed by the architect Amos Faulkner in 1899–1905 for the Eton College Estate adjoining Primrose Hill in Hampstead are typical of the prosperous middle-class residences built in such places. Faulkner's designs are extremely varied, adapting the styles of numerous eminent architects such as Norman Shaw, Stokes, Ernest George, Voysey and others in houses spread around Elsworthy Road, Wadham Gardens, Eton Avenue and elsewhere.

Fig. 28   Detail of entrance and iron railings, No. 38 Cheyne Walk, Chelsea (1899–1901) by C. R. Ashbee.

It is the new outer suburbs of London, however, which are more typical of the period. Their major period of growth started almost precisely in 1900, for at that time a general rise in wages, and in the number of clerical jobs available in London, coincided with the harnessing of electricity as power for public transport. For the first time, many central London workers could afford a house in green surroundings and could be transported there from their work within one hour.[6] It was a potent dream in the Edwardian mind, much stimulated by the press and by advertising.

The economic background in Britain of 1900, outlined in chapter one, is significant. By then a considerable part of the urban population was enjoying a prosperity it had never known before, despite the continuing poverty of the deprived people lower down the financial scale.

The increase in city jobs was particularly marked in London. In terms of political history, the state was intervening in more areas of life than before. More responsibilities meant more jobs, and the staff of national and local government grew immensely. The years around 1900 saw the start of insurance as the giant business it later became, partly due to legislation and partly to increased consciousness of the importance of financial security among ordinary people. So here and in commerce in general, business developments meant more clerical jobs offering reasonable salaries.

Better jobs aroused higher expectations. Writing in 1907, M. Kaufman[7] noted,

> A secondary cause (of inner city slums) is the ... removal of the better class of inhabitants ... to the suburbs. Formerly these exercised a refining and elevating influence on their less-favoured neighbours. But since their removal to their country residences, the inner circle of London has become, in the words of Lord Rosebery, 'a great desert inhabited by neglected humanity' who sink lower and lower.

Yet those able to move to greener places could hardly be blamed for doing so. The environment in much inner London housing was bleak. 'There were many streets where even gas was unknown', wrote Thomas Burke[8] of the years around 1900. 'The people in those streets spent their evenings with lamp and candle light, and all cooking throughout the year had to be done by coal fire. The houses were just boxes. Bathrooms were unknown and fittings, other than fireplaces and a cupboard or two,

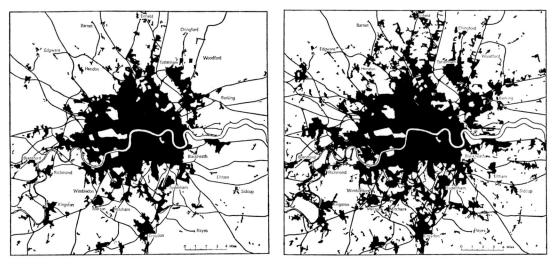

Fig. 29   The growth of London's outer suburbs 1901–1911.

Fig. 30 Suburban terraced 'half-houses' (one household upstairs, another downstairs), in Warner Road, off Pretoria Avenue, Walthamstow (1905). Each porch contains two front doors, a standard feature on the Warner Estate and the Winn Estate.

were unthought of.'

It was electrified public transport which made the great expansion possible. Its growth will be recounted in more detail in chapter six, but the general situation in 1900 must be summarised here. During the nineteenth century a fair network of steam-powered railways above the ground had been built to connect London with its few outer suburbs, while the Metropolitan Railway, for all the dirt and fumes of its steam engines, provided the first underground. The Great Central Railway was built in the 1890s, but by then the railway-building boom above ground was over, partly because the cost of London land was by then too expensive. There was an extensive service of slow horse-drawn buses and trams, but these could not travel to places more than eight miles from Charing Cross in a time acceptable to suburban commuters.

London's first electric underground railway of any length, the Central Line, opened in 1900, but this and the other Tubes did not reach the outer suburbs for several years. It was the electric trams from 1900 onwards, the motor bus after 1906 and only after 1910 the underground Tube trains which brought the estate agents, the developers and the building contractors flocking to places further out than Golders Green, than West Ham and than Streatham. Between 1901 and 1911, Acton increased its population by 52 per cent to 57 500, Chingford by 86 per cent, Hendon by 73 per cent, Barnes by 71 per cent and Merton and Morden by 156 per cent.

Not all these new suburbs were middle-class paradises, for it is perhaps surprising how effectively open-market capitalism zoned the new housing estates for different social classes. Thus the Warner Estate and the Winn Estate around Pretoria Avenue and Forest Road in Walthamstow, both built in 1905, are rather depressing rows of 'half-houses' (one family upstairs, another downstairs) for comparatively poor families.[9]

Nevertheless, the standard of accommodation and design of houses did improve over the years, partly following the plans by experimental and talented architects illustrated in the building press. Golders Green is an example which shows this development. The extension of the electric Underground Railway's Northern Line to Golders Green was authorised by Parliament in 1902, the tunnels were built by 1906 and the line opened in June 1907 – one of the first Tubes to reach an undeveloped suburb. By the autumn of 1906 two adventurous estate agents had set up business in wooden huts on what was still open countryside. The price of land rose from about £250 per acre to £1000 per acre, and £5500 for areas suitable for shops near the station. Early houses were white roughcast, with their gables sometimes half-timbered. Most were semi-detached, but some were free-standing or terraced. In most of the frontage designs the influence of Voysey, Ashbee or Baillie Scott is evident. Building contractors made fortunes and lost them, some ending in the bankruptcy court. Others, such as Edward Streather and William Turner, went on to build thousands of houses, moving on to Hendon when Golders Green was filling up. These commercial developments did the minimum necessary to make their estates seem a realisation of the suburban dream. There were gardens and the houses were reminiscent of country cottages, but the road lay-out was dull and as many plots as possible were packed into each acre.[10]

Figs. 31–34   Houses in Golders Gardens, Wessex Gardens and Woodstock Avenue, Golders Green (*c*.1907–08) architects unknown.

The dream came much nearer to reality with the acquisition in 1906 of 243 acres of Golders Green by the Hampstead Garden Suburb Trust, inspired by the magnate of charitable work and social reform, Dame Henrietta Barnett. Mrs Barnett, as she was then, was an enthusiast for the garden city movement of her acquaintance Ebenezer Howard and was determined to provide a new model for future suburbs. She engaged the architect Raymond Unwin, town-planner of the slightly earlier Letchworth Garden City, to design the lay-out of Hampstead Garden Suburb. Unwin produced the plan, with curving roads around and beyond Hampstead Heath Extension, a central green with two churches and an institute building for community activities. Apart from individual houses and terraces, small cul-de-sac streets off the main roads led to secluded low blocks of flats around central courtyards.

Many of the architects engaged at Hampstead Garden Suburb were leading figures in the Arts and Crafts movement and produced designs of much charm and restrained originality. Further out of London, such architects built individual houses which set standards for their locality. Often the influence of Voysey can be seen, as in the design for a house at Bromley by Niven and Wigglesworth exhibited at the Royal Academy in 1900. Voysey himself built a celebrated suburban house for his own family in the same year. This is the Orchard in Shire Lane, Chorley Wood. The widespread publication of the design led to its adaptation as a model for numerous

Fig. 35   Houses at Nos. 9 and 10 Meadway, Hampstead Garden Suburb (*c.*1909).
Colour plate 1.   Detail of entrance, Annesley Lodge, Hampstead (1896) by C. F. A. Voysey.

semi-detached suburban houses all over England and even in outposts of the British Empire. Another distinguished domestic architect was M. H. Baillie Scott (1865–1945). Baillie Scott was clearly influenced by Voysey at the beginning of the century before his own individual manner emerged. But even in his design of *c.*1902 for a London suburban house at Hurlingham, the proportions and detailing are more personal than those by most other followers of Voysey.

Inside these Edwardian suburban houses of artistic pretensions, the spaces were usually lighter and less cluttered with furniture than their predecessors. Most architects designed flat ceilings, often with beams revealed, but occasionally a graceful vaulting was used. An example of this is the entrance hall of The Leys in Barnet Lane, Elstree, designed in 1901 by George Walton (1867–1933). Walton was a Scot who studied design at the Glasgow School of Art and became a friend of Charles Rennie Mackintosh, before moving to London in 1898. His closeness to Mackintosh can be detected in some of his fireplace designs and, more startlingly, in the fittings and screen of the billiard room in The Leys.

Walton's interiors were graceful and sophisticated. Other eminent architects sought a more rustic look in their houses further out around London, as in a luxuriously simple dining room designed in 1901 by Sir Edwin Lutyens (1869–1944) or in the living room of about 1900 with furniture and plasterwork by the architect–

Fig. 36   Voysey: The Orchard (for himself), Chorley Wood (1900–01).
Colour plate 2.   Wallpaper 'The Meadow' with 'The May Tree' frieze (1903) by Walter Crane.

52

Fig. 37 (*Upper left*)   Fireplace for a small house (1890s) designed by M. H. Baillie Scott.
Fig. 38 (*Upper centre*)   Dining room (1901) by Sir Edwin Lutyens.
Fig. 39   Billiard Room, The Leys, Elstree (1901) by George Walton.

Fig. 40 (*Upper right*)   Detail of central house in multiple house block, south-east corner of Meadway and Hampstead Way, Hampstead Garden Suburb (1908–09) by M. H. Baillie Scott.
Fig. 41   Living room with furniture and plasterwork designed by Ernest Gimson (c.1900).

craftsman Ernest Gimson (1864–1920). The contrasts of taste in furnishing by individual Arts and Crafts designers is again neatly demonstrated by two sideboards of *c.*1903. One, by Walton, is of slender elegance combined with a firm overall composition. The other, Gimson's sideboard of oak, is powerful and masculine in composition and detailing. Only in decorative work, such as wallpapers and fabrics or metalwork fittings and furnishings, was the curling linear side of Arts and Crafts design found, unlike the Art Nouveau architecture of continental Europe, whose tendrils entered the very structure of many buildings.

Upstairs in the stylish Arts and Crafts house, the bedrooms would usually show the same simplicity of line relieved by bands or other touches of curvilinear decoration, as seen in the bedrooms designed by the talented design team of Messrs. Liberty and Company. Designers such as George Walton were also quite equal to clients' demands for delicate feminine prettiness when the occasion arose.

In 1908, it was still a matter for special approving note that an estate of new houses in Golders Green all had a bath and an upstairs W.C. But in fairly costly suburban houses, the Edwardian bathroom often had a glory all of its own, with hip-baths, baths with showers and wash-basin units of great character, though often lacking refinement.

Weekday life in most of these suburban houses was extremely busy after the husband left for work. There were no labour-saving electrical devices and a huge amount of cleaning was needed to keep house and decorations shining. Most of the laundry, with clothes of great complexity, was done within the household. Meals were large and heavy, and required much preparation. If the husband earned £150 a year, a smallish suburban house and one maid to help the wife were considered normal. After 1910, domestic help was harder to find as more women were employed

Fig. 42   Bedroom (*c.*1900) designed by L. Wyburd, E. P. Roberts and A. Denington, designers for Liberty and Co.

as low-paid clerks. As for local amenities, small shops sprang up patchily in the first few years in the allotted places on each new estate. The banks, however, were quick to see the possibilities, and many London suburbs have attractive small branch offices, usually designed in a warm and friendly Neo-Georgian style.

In the new suburbs of 1900 to 1905 there was little entertainment outside the home. There were twenty-three theatres in the London suburbs, but none of them further from the centre than Camberwell in the south or Holloway Road in the north.[11] Music halls were far from harmonious with the respectable image which suburban dwellers had of themselves, but evening gatherings for songs around the piano in the home were a widespread institution. From 1906 onwards the cinema started to appear, with silent movies shown at first in small hired rooms, later in specially constructed buildings. By 1912 there were over 500 cinemas in London and its suburbs. Although A. H. Beavan reported[12] in 1901 that 'almost every borough in London has now its Public Library', he was referring to the inner suburbs. Those suburbs which grew up in the Edwardian decade often had to depend on the small commercial lending libraries for their literature. In 1908 there was a great fashion for roller-skating and a number of suburban rinks were built during the three years of the craze. During the summer, there were tennis clubs and *thé-dansants*. And there was always the possibility of going for a walk through tree-lined streets bordered by gardens. On Sundays such walks were taken in best clothes after church and Sunday dinner, for the Edwardian Sabbath was a serious affair.

One may wonder how reality compared with cherished fantasy for most of those tens of thousands of families who used their new prosperity to escape from the crowded houses and smoke of central London between 1900 and 1914. Contemporary accounts make it clear that they did not find the garden paradise which Ebenezer

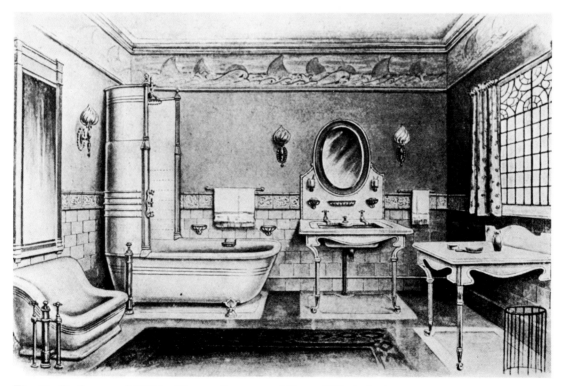

Fig. 43   Bathroom of 1904 by Messrs. Beavan and Sons of Westminster.

Howard's books, the articles in the newspapers and the estate agents' advertisements had made them hope for. But if they had chosen their suburb and their house carefully, they at least lived in lighter and more spacious rooms with cleaner air and plants and trees around them. And if they chose, as many did, to clutter those rooms with furniture and ornaments as if Voysey and Ashbee had never existed, they were probably happier with such cosy surroundings than with space and simplicity.

The story of this chapter has traced the spread of the new simple white type of Arts and Crafts house from the early works of Voysey and Ashbee out into the suburbs of

Fig. 44   No. 81 Wimpole Street, Marylebone (1891) by Sir Frank Elgood. One of a sequence of designs by Elgood on the Howard de Walden estate, showing the development of the Neo-Georgian town house.
Fig. 45.   No. 39 Harley Street (1893–94) by Elgood.

the 1900s. But the Arts and Crafts architects in general moved in a different direction in their houses in central London. There was good reason for this. The dominant strain of architectural ideas within the movement had always held that originality in design should be rooted in the vernacular local manner. As far as London was concerned, there were few examples of good quality domestic building earlier than 1670 still to be seen by the end of the nineteenth century. In effect, the vernacular tradition was that of the solid brick houses of Georgian times, with a sparing use of Classical detailing. For rather grander houses, the Georgian tradition prescribed

Fig. 46   No. 11 Welbeck Street, Marylebone (1905) by Elgood.
Fig. 47   No. 32 Weymouth Street, Marylebone (1911) by Elgood.

stone, either in Classical dressings and decoration or even in entirely stone-fronted designs. By 1900, a number of architects were building London houses in styles derived from the Georgian, which evolved naturally enough from the 'Queen Anne' style of 1870–90 – just as English Baroque emerged from eclecticism for larger buildings.

Big town houses by Fairfax Wade and, later, by Lutyens in the Neo-Georgian manner will be described in the next chapter. Here an account must be given of the more usual middle-sized house in central London. Examples can be found by Horace Field, Walter Cave, W. D. Caröe, Detmar Blow and others, but the most illuminating series is perhaps the nineteen houses built by Sir Frank Elgood around Harley Street, Marylebone, on the Howard de Walden and Portman estates between 1891 and 1913. Elgood's contribution to urban Neo-Georgian design in London has been overlooked until now – his standard of design was steady, and occasionally he produced a work of outstanding quality.[13] The earliest of his Marylebone houses are of brick in the Queen Anne mixed style; No. 9 Harley Street and the attractively simple No. 81 Wimpole Street both date from 1891. But the handsome pair of the same year, Nos. 41 and 42 Devonshire Street, are Classical designs in stone, with a few features – such as the window proportions – still reminiscent of the Queen Anne.

A bold change followed in 1893–94 when Elgood built No. 39 Harley Street. This is a successful freely Classical design of stone and brick, with an extended Venetian window on the first floor. The basic source is clearly, at several points, Norman Shaw's No. 170 Queen's Gate, Kensington, of 1887–88, but Elgood brings it off well in this very different sort of house. There followed the pretty Neo-Georgian double house at Nos. 8 and 10 Wigmore Street in 1896, with shallow bays below and strange squashed Venetian windows above, and the vigorous Baroque blocked surrounds of the windows. Elgood added Baroque windows to the older No. 49 Harley Street in 1898, but before examining more of these houses it will be useful to look at the ideas behind the style he employed.

Elgood is interesting for more than his own designs. In 1898, he made one of the clearest statements on record[14] about the intentions behind the contemporary Baroque and Neo-Georgian movements. He saw them as the logical development from the 'Queen Anne' style, which had recently turned into a manner closer to 'the style that was practised in the time of Queen Anne and the early Georges with all its modifications and variations'. After that time, Elgood felt, the imported Palladianism of Lord Burlington had robbed our architecture of its freshness and its English character.

> It is only natural that architects should hark back to the time when architecture in England was on the progressive wane, and attempt to start afresh from the point when inventive genius gave place to mere copyism ... The possibilities of the style seem infinite, and there is plenty of evidence that those who have the fortune to build in it are not trammelled with precedents and hard-and-fast lines. And yet the effect is generally quiet and pleasing, has a thoroughly English appearance and is entirely suited to modern requirements. But ... this is not imitation of a past style. There is a wonderful originality in such designs and an entire absence of similarity or copying ... who can say that it may not lead to what must be the desire of us all, namely the formulating of a truly English twentieth century progressive architecture?

Much of this originality within the Neo-Georgian style – which was widely practised in London by fine architects such as Lutyens, Field, Adshead, Dawber and Arnold Mitchell by about this time – is seen in what is perhaps the best of Elgood's

Marylebone houses, No. 11 Welbeck Street of 1905. Here a vigorous composition in brick and stone with Baroque detailing mounts to a hipped gable as powerful as Ashbee's simple white roofline at No. 39 Cheyne Walk. Of the dozen or so Marylebone houses that followed, the joyous No. 34 Weymouth Street (1908), Nos. 70–74 Wigmore Street (1908), the identical Nos. 24 and 32 Weymouth Street (1911) and the smooth grey stone No. 85 Wimpole Street (1913) show the variety of Elgood's Neo-Georgian designs. Finally, Radiant House at Nos. 34–38 Mortimer Street was done in 1915 in partnership with P. L. Pither. Here the architects take off into strange Mannerist forms and use the colourful shiny glazed exteriors which we will meet again in Ricardo's work in the next chapter.

5 Mansion Blocks and Mansions

In the year 1907 the architect and writer W. Shaw Sparrow remarked[1] on the 'boom in flats some years ago'. He went on to say that

> members of the middle classes are called upon to keep up a position more or less beyond their means, because they can afford still less the danger either of living in a way that might stamp them as failures, or of dressing in a style that their clients or employers might regard as too negligent or too poor. This fact no architect should forget when designing a block of flats for the middle classes. His building should have style. It must not be second-rate in workmanship; none who looks at it from the outside should be able to guess that the rents are low.

The boom in the building of flats in London started slowly in the 1870s, although blocks had been built earlier, and gathered momentum until the period between 1897 and the construction slump of 1906 saw dozens of large mansion blocks rising in all fashionable parts of the city and inner suburbs. In the passage quoted, Shaw Sparrow pointed to one of the reasons why London followed Paris and Edinburgh's long-established liking for middle-class flats. With their rising prosperity, these classes wanted a new environment. Prices for building land near the centre were increasing quickly enough to make new houses prohibitive. So their choice lay between a move to the new suburbs, as shown in the previous chapter, and a move into a block of flats nearer the West End. As well as apartments large enough for a family, the period around 1900 saw the construction of a considerable number of blocks of small bachelor flats right in the centre – though most of these have in their turn become too expensive for their original purpose and have been converted into offices.

The architects and developers of these flats gave much thought to the expectations of likely tenants. If the users were thought likely to have advanced artistic tastes, the inventive Free Style drawn from the Arts and Crafts movement was acceptable. This manner can be seen in the large block called Manor House on the corner of Marylebone Road and Lisson Grove (1903 by Gordon and Gunton), the Chambers on the corner of Piccadilly and Bond Street (1905 by Read and Macdonald) and the two remarkable blocks in Jermyn Street, No. 112 of 1900 and Nos. 70–72 of 1902–03, by Reginald Morphew. Morphew's interiors are finely decorated and detailed in a manner close to that of Voysey or Baillie Scott. Scott himself built a notably delicate block of apartments a little later, and further out from the centre – this was Waterlow Court of 1908–09, small flats for professional women at Hampstead Garden Suburb.

Most of the designers of mansion blocks built around 1900, however, recognised that their users would want grandeur and opulence before anything else. And at that time grandeur meant the Edwardian Baroque style made fashionable by many town

Fig. 48 Affluent display in the entrance hall of a mansion block of flats, Blomfield Court, Maida Vale in 1904, designed by Boehmer and Gibbs.

Fig. 49 ´ Gordon and Gunton: Manor House (flats), Marylebone Road (1903) by Gordon and Gunton. The composition of the block is striking and the walls are decorated with Arts and Crafts motifs.
Fig. 50   Living-room fireplace in a flat, Marlborough Chambers, 70 Jermyn Street, St James's (1902–03) by Reginald Morphew. The design shows a simplified vigour comparable with contemporary work by Charles Rennie Mackintosh in Glasgow.

Fig. 51   Baillie Scott: the courtyard, Waterlow Court, Heath Close, off Hampstead Way, Hampstead Garden Suburb (1908–09). The housing block was built for working ladies. It had a communal dining room and other shared facilities.
Fig. 52   Mansion block of flats, No. 12 Hyde Park Place, Bayswater Road, near Marble Arch (1903) by Frank Verity. Luxury flats in the French style.
Fig. 53   Drawing-room in a flat, No. 12 Hyde Park Place, Marble Arch (1903) by Frank Verity.

hall and government buildings designed from 1897 onwards, or a French Classical manner after 1904, while opulence meant spaciousness and rich architectural detail. The entrance and approaches to each flat were of great importance to tenants 'called upon to keep up a position more or less beyond their means' and this accounts for the amount of space devoted to Edwardian entrance halls and staircases which often appear wasteful to modern eyes. Frank Verity, one of the most successful architects of these grand blocks of flats, wrote[2]

> It should be our aim to design a plan having few corridors … (which cost) as much to build as if the same space were allotted to rooms … The main entrance and staircase should form a central architectural feature, the importance of which does not appear to have been sufficiently appreciated … tenants when they leave their flats seldom ring for the lift; they walk down the stairs; and for this reason, among others, the staircase should be of ample dimensions and designed to create a good impression … In every flat … it is advisable that the drawing-room or morning-room should be entered from the vestibule, without it being necessary for us to cross the lounge.

In his apartment blocks such as No. 12 Hyde Park Place (1903) and No. 25 Berkeley Square (1904), Verity certainly lived up to his own standards of planning, although

Fig. 54   Harley House mansion block, Marylebone Road, near Regent's Park (1903–04) by Boehmer and Gibbs.

few other Edwardian architects followed his advice to eliminate corridors.

Verity's apartment buildings can be found in the Marble Arch, Mayfair and St James's areas of central London, favourite positions for luxurious mansion blocks. Another prosperous architect, Paul Hoffman, built flats in Mayfair – No. 15 Hanover Square and Harewood House in Hanover Square of *c*.1900 are good examples of his rather French type of Baroque – but also further out in Kensington, where the huge St George's Terrace in Gloucester Road and Alexandra Court in Queen's Gate were erected at much the same time. To the north, Regent's Park and St John's Wood were favoured, too. The architects Boehmer and Gibbs put up big buildings with comfortable flats inside, but messy Baroque exteriors, such as Harley House (between Marylebone Road and Regent's Park) and Sandringham Court in Maida Vale. On the north side of the park a more distinguished architect, Sir Frank Elgood, built the large block called North Gate in an English Baroque style on the corner of Prince of Wales Road and St John's Wood High Street in 1901 and E. P. Warren built Hanover House nearby in 1904. Later in the Edwardian decade, economy together with Verity's increasing preference for Parisian styles and a general movement among architects towards purer Classicism, gradually ended the popularity of the extravagant Baroque manner. More disciplined designs followed, such as Verity's

Fig. 55   Upper landing with wall paintings at No. 26 Grosvenor Square, Mayfair in 1902. Designed by Howard and Sons and other decorators co-ordinated by Duveen Brothers for the art collector G. A. Cooper.

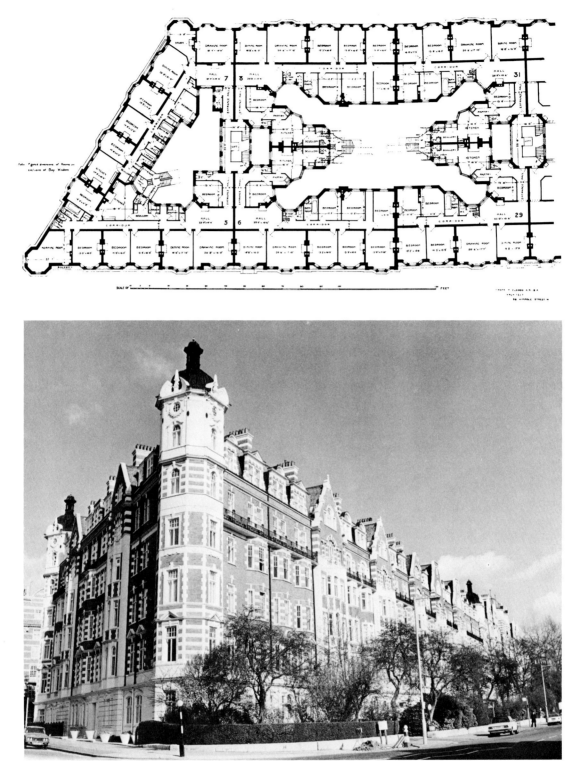

Fig. 56   Plan of North Gate, Prince Albert Road, Regent's Park (1902–03) by Sir Frank Elgood.
Fig. 57   North Gate mansion flats, Prince Albert Road, Regent's Park (1901) by Sir Frank Elgood. The English Baroque style in a large block of flats, with Arts and Crafts detailing in the metalwork of the balconies.
Colour plate 3.   Debenham House, Holland Park (1905–07) by Halsey Ricardo.

own No. 7 Cleveland Row beside St James's Palace and Blow and Billerey's Nos. 44–50 Park Street in Mayfair (1911–12).

This same movement brought to an end the innovative style of interior decoration and furnishing seen in Morphew's St James's apartments. If the architectural styles of most other mansion blocks drew their character from one or another kind of Classicism, so did the typical interiors. Living rooms could be in any one of a dozen Classical manners from Wren to Adam or even to French Neo-Classical in that age of the Entente Cordiale and a Francophile king. In the furniture, the Victorian 'dust-catching flounces and furbelows', so loathed by Voysey and other Arts and Crafts architects, had largely gone, but middle-class taste moved towards Adam-like delicacy rather than novel forms. Often the living rooms were crammed with ornaments, but an increased liking for space did sometimes show itself there and in the bedrooms.

Less change of taste could be seen amongst the really wealthy, either in the occasional new London mansions built for them about 1900 or in the contemporary redecorations of their older houses. The sudden rise to prominence of numerous fashionable interior decorators in London in the 1890s, many of them ladies, so well described by Nicholas Cooper in *The Opulent Eye*,[3] led to a wilder variety of decorative styles than had been known before. Such schemes as that of 1902 by various decorators supervised by the art dealers Duveen Bros. for Mr G. A. Cooper (later Sir George) at 26 Grosvenor Square were understandable enough for a wealthy art-collector, but designs such as Mr J. C. Moreton Thompson's drawing room at 56 Hans Place in 1898 or the Turkish bathroom of 1904 at Moray Lodge in Campden Hill give rise to a fond nostalgia for past spendthrift luxuriance.

The rise of the City of London in banking, insurance and international finance during the 1890s brought up a new wave of London millionaires, some of them close friends of King Edward VII. But these rich bankers rarely spent their fortunes on building new houses in London, preferring to refurbish older mansions or to build more expansively in the countryside. As a result there are not very many really large houses of the Edwardian period in town. One of the major exceptions is the tremendous Baroque mansion in Mayfair built by Fairfax Wade for Lord Windsor on the corner of Mount Street and Park Street in 1897, the Jubilee year when English Baroque suddenly became a fashionable success and the year after the design of Wade's more individualistic houses at Nos. 63 and 64 Sloane Street. Mayfair, largely owned by the Duke of Westminster, was to receive a number of large new houses and blocks of flats around Park Street during the next few years, many by Detmar Blow[4] (or his partner Fernand Billerey) who became the Duke's favoured architect early in the century.

Eight years after the building of Lord Windsor's house, work started on the most splendid of all Edwardian mansions in London. This is the Debenham House at No. 8 Addison Road in Holland Park, built for the department store millionaire Ernest Debenham in 1905–07. Its architect was Halsey Ricardo (1854–1928), a leading figure in the Arts and Crafts movement, whose other works consist only of a few good houses and a huge railway station in Calcutta.

The Debenham House is extraordinary in many ways. In one sense it expresses the recognition by the Arts and Crafts movement that the English domestic adaptation of Classical architecture in Georgian times was as valid as any other style to be used as a traditional vernacular starting point for modern building design. Other leading

Colour plate 4.   Interior, the London Coliseum (1902–04) by Frank Matcham.

Arts and Crafts designers' work was used by Ricardo in decorating the house. The lovely tiles inside and outside were by Ricardo's former partner William de Morgan, the plasterwork by Ernest Gimson, while glass produced by Edward Prior was used in internal doors. The rooms inside the house are fine spaces with much rich colouring, especially the central hall – although its spectacular ceiling mosaic was not part of Ricardo's plan.

Yet the style of the Debenham house cannot really be called Neo-Georgian, as that manner is generally seen. The detailing, though not the overall composition, is developed from Italian Renaissance architecture rather than an English Classicism. Most exotic of all, the walls recessed behind the pinkish terracotta Classical detailing of the exterior are of a shiny glazed brick, a mellow green on the ground floor, a brilliant blue above. The use of shiny self-cleaning surfaces, tile and glazed brick, was a long-standing passion of Ricardo's as a way of providing colourful building surfaces suitable for London's dirty climate. He had given several talks on the subject and the Debenham House was his great chance to demonstrate his idea. Ricardo's self-cleaning theory is successful to this day on the house, but it was taken up by only a few other architects.[5]

Fig. 58   The Turkish bathroom, Moray Lodge, Campden Hill in 1904. Designed by Goldsmith.
Fig. 59   House for Lord Windsor, Mount Street, Mayfair (1896–97) by Fairfax Wade. A rare example of a Baroque town mansion of the time.

Fig. 60 Halsey Ricardo: fireplace in drawing room, Debenham House, 8 Addison Road, North Kensington, London (1905–07). Various marbles and a band of De Morgan tiles under the shallow arch. Ceiling plasterwork by Ernest Gimson.

Fig. 61 Edwin Lutyens: No. 7 St James's Square, London (1911). The design, with only cornice and porch giving any depth to the elevation's surface, is moving towards the Stripped Classicism of the following twenty years.

Fig. 62 Two houses in Great Peter Street (known as No. 8 Little College Street and No. 11 Cowley Street), near Smith Square, Westminster (1912) by Sir Edwin Lutyens.

There are many other Edwardian houses of a considerable size in London including excellent works by Balfour and Turner, Romaine Walker, and rebuilt interiors by Blow and Billerey and by Belcher and Joass. But there are no other really vast mansions built before 1914 of an architectural interest to compare with those of Lord Windsor and of Ernest Debenham, except a series built by Sir Edwin Lutyens in 1911 and 1912. Of these, No. 7 St James's Square shows Lutyens moving towards a Classical manner stripped of all decoration on the storeys between the entrance porch and the cornice; he and other architects were to use this sort of frontage on many office buildings after the Great War of 1914–18. In the same year, 1911, he built the pretty Neo-Georgian house at No. 36 Smith Square, Westminster, and then in 1912, a pair of very large houses near Smith Square in Great Peter Street. This pair, known as No. 8 Little College Street and No. 11 Cowley Street, form a single grand composition of great simplicity in a Neo-Georgian style, with a splendid hipped roof. These buildings are the earliest private houses which Lutyens built in central London, though all four have been converted into offices since then. They are strong designs, worthy of the great architect at his best and developing the extraordinary play with Classical detailing which he was to continue all his life.

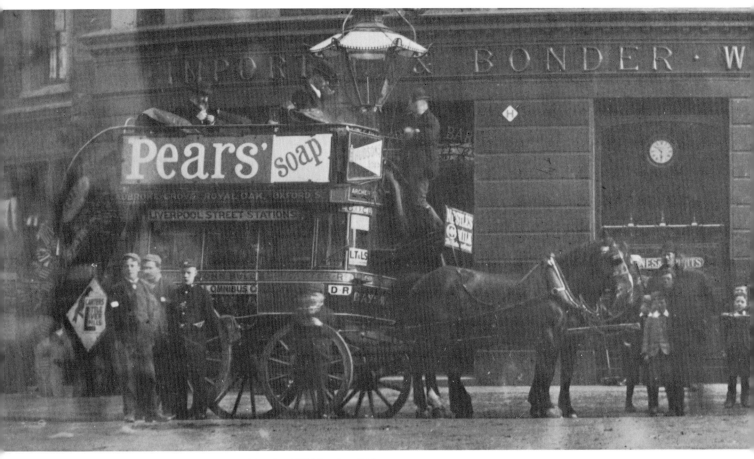

Fig. 63   Horse buses in Notting Hill in the 1890s.

6 Getting to Work – Public Transport

Public transport, and particularly electrically powered public transport, was probably the most important single cause of the extensive changes between 1900 and 1910 in the places where many Londoners lived. The rule of thumb was that commuters found it intolerable to travel for more than one hour from their homes to their places of work, and only where there were railway lines was it possible to do a journey of more than six miles in that time.

The first London railway had opened in 1838 from Bricklayers' Arms to Greenwich. By 1880 there were 350 railway stations in central and suburban London, with lines radiating from the central termini. From 1863 onwards, the Metropolitan gave London its first underground railway, but its passengers coughed and choked from the fumes of the steam engines in its tunnels. These railways allowed suburbs to grow out in lines from the city but between the radii there were still only horse-drawn buses and trams during the 1890s. And for many commuters working in the middle of

London, the trams did not come close to their places of work. A. H. Beavan[1] wrote in 1901:

> One has to go across Westminster Bridge or ... as far west as Hammersmith or Shepherd's Bush, to get in touch with the great system of tram-lines. The bringing of these lines to the centre of London has always been ... rigorously and successfully opposed ... on the plea that it lowers the character of the thoroughfare and injures the vehicles that cross its rails.

Many suburban dwellers therefore had no choice but to use the horsedrawn buses which had become a large commercial concern since the first was put on London streets from the Yorkshire Stingo public house to the Bank by a Mr Shillibeer in 1829. In 1856 the London General Omnibus Company started to buy out other bus companies and by 1900 it owned about 1300 out of the 3000 horse-drawn buses and trams carrying an estimated 500 million passengers a year in Greater London.[2]

> On the journey citywards, they start as early as 7.10 a.m. from Putney ... 7.25 from Kilburn. The last bus (from Liverpool Street in the City) leaving for Kilburn at 11.40 p.m. ... Putney 12.14 p.m. ... The men's hours are long; even on Sundays they average $12\frac{1}{2}$ hours ... Some men get a Sunday off work every fortnight.

Another writer[3] recalled,

> The horse-bus driver was in touch with his front-seat passengers and they could talk to him. Londoners then were not over-sensitive to wind and rain, and the open top of the bus gave them a view of the world through which they rumbled ... Men who lived in the suburbs and went every day to the City got to know their bus-driver, and their front seat was always reserved for them. If they were not at the corner when their bus stopped, the bus would wait for them.

For the more prosperous there were of course horse-drawn cabs of variable standards in 1900.

> It is difficult to explain why, in the world's Metropolis, comfortable and comely four-wheeled cabs, well-horsed and driven by decently clad men, cannot be had. There are still far too many crazy old 'growlers' whose frames are afflicted with innumerable gaps, chinks and crevices, and which are neither wind nor water-tight, while their horses are miserable creatures.[4]

Yet 1900 saw the start of sweeping changes in public transport and the same writer continued. 'It is true there are a few electric cabs, some with a door at one side which look like truncated omnibuses.' Electricity and the petrol engine were to revolutionise all types of London public transport within the following decade, pushing into oblivion other experiments such as the L.C.C.'s brief attempt in 1905–07 to use the Thames as a water highway, with steamers doing the work of buses.

The classic account of this revolution is contained in one of the most distinguished works of modern historical scholarship, *A History of London Transport*, by T. C. Barker and Michael Robbins.[5] Barker and Robbins trace the rapid growth of 12 000 miles of electric tramways in the United States of America in the seven years after the first tram ran in 1888 at Richmond, Virginia. A small length of tramway opened in England in Leeds in 1891 and Bristol operated a considerable tramway from 1895 onwards, but the first electric tramway in London only started in April 1901, in the western suburbs. From then on, the London tramways grew rapidly and

Fig. 64   Horse trams at the Archway Tavern, Islington in the 1890s.

Fig. 65   Excavating the Great Northern and City Tube Railway, 1901. Men at work in the Greathead Shield.
Fig. 66   Filigree panel in an Arts and Crafts decorative style (1905–06), above a lift at Covent Garden underground station on the Piccadilly Line. The architect to the Underground Electric Railways Ltd company was Leslie W. Green.

were in time taken over by the London County Council. They only had the roads to themselves for a few years, for in 1905 the first motor-buses appeared in London streets (some years after the first private cars) and the long struggle between bus and tram started, finally resulting in victory for the buses fifty years later. Traffic grew enormously as the suburbs expanded – thus, in the year 1903 there were an estimated 394 million journeys on trams and 287 million on horse-buses, while in 1910 there were 764 million journeys on trams and 377 million on buses of both kinds.[6] The London United Tramways Ltd lines extended rapidly enough for them to build their own generating station building at Chiswick, designed by W. Curtis Green in 1904, in a handsome Neo-Georgian style. Shortly afterwards, in 1906, the London County Council built a generating station in Greenwich for their tramways.

The electric trams were excluded from central London for several years after 1900 and it was precisely there that the electric underground railway, or tube, started its growth. As early as 1891, the Central London Railway Company obtained permission from Parliament to build an underground railway from the Bank, in the City, to Shepherd's Bush in the west, where the suburban trams started. The Central Line tunnels were bored through the earth with the Greathead Shield, rather than using the surface cut-and-cover technique of the old Metropolitan, and London's first tube (apart from some very short earlier sections of the Northern Line) was opened by the Prince of Wales on 27 July 1900. It ran from Mansion House to Shepherd's Bush with the intervening stations still used on the middle stretch of the Central Line today. It was acclaimed at the time. 'The cars on the Electric Central are an improvement on any yet ... You can see to read in them ... the carriages are luxuriously upholstered ... So far (1901), the railway has been a decided success, the daily average of travellers by it being about 150 000.'[7]

The success of this and the other early tube lines was largely due to the energy and determination of an extraordinary American engineer–financier, Charles T. Yerkes, whose Underground Electric Railways Ltd took over the half-born projects of a number of other stumbling companies. The Northern Line was authorised by Parliament in 1892 and 1893; the Angel–Bank–Clapham stretch opened in 1901, the Charing Cross–Euston–Golders Green branch in 1907. The line from Waterloo to Baker Street was also approved in 1893; after a bankruptcy the U.E.R.L. took it over and it opened in 1906, to be dubbed the 'Bakerloo' line by press and public immediately. The first part of the Piccadilly Line, from Kensington to Piccadilly and on to King's Cross, was started in 1902 and opened in 1906. Only after these basic foundations had been laid did the underground railways push out into the further suburbs where the great mass of middle-class commuters lived, offering them an alternative to the trams. Yerkes died in 1905 of Bright's Disease, leaving this great legacy to Londoners.

In 1900 the City and South London Railway Company, which had run the first underground, built new head offices at No. 75 Moorgate, in the City. This building by T. Phillips Figgis, in a free Arts and Crafts style, is one of the most charming of its date (Figgis did a number of other stations for the company).

The architectural style of the ordinary underground stations of the early 1900s is a familiar feature of the London scene, though some of the stations have inevitably been rebuilt over the years. They are among the few examples of street architecture which took up Halsey Ricardo's ideas about the use of shiny glazed bricks and tiles on street façades, using a rather heavy ox-blood reddish brown. All employ the generally Classical style thought suitable for almost any public buildings at the time, but many still retain metalwork fittings in the Arts and Crafts free manner of the period (e.g. Covent Garden on the Piccadilly Line and Holland Park Station on the Central Line). The original Central Line stations of 1900 were designed by Delissa Joseph. The architect to the U.E.R.L. for the Northern, Bakerloo and Piccadilly Line stations of 1903–10 was Leslie W. Green (born 1874). During the years 1895–99 many stations were also rebuilt on the Inner Circle Line (Metropolitan and District) by the architect George Sherrin; these included High Street Kensington, Gloucester Road, South Kensington, Temple and Monument. The architect to the Metropolitan Railway at this time, was Charles W. Clark, who designed several of their stations of the 1900s as well as their head offices of 1912 behind Baker Street station.

A very different type of building for the U.E.R.L. was the huge power station which it built in 1902 at Lots Road in Chelsea, close to the Thames for the barges of coal for the generators providing electric current to the company's four underground lines.

It was not only the underground railway that was involved with electricity. Some of the older railways running out of London were soon affected by electrification. In 1901 it was reported that

> Waterloo has taken on a new lease of life ... by means of its electric railway (the short independent tube from Waterloo to the Bank, known as 'The Drain'). For many years a mere shed propped up by arches, it has been added to bit by bit until it is now in extent inferior only to Liverpool Street; but this evolutionary process has left it an ungainly bulk with little or no definite plan.[8]

Fig. 67   People waiting for the lifts at the Bank underground station on the Central Line in 1901.

The owners, the London and South Western Railway, decided in 1900 to start rebuilding with a grand Classical stone façade around the new sheds. This took twenty-two years to complete, for the company financed the work out of its profits, and the station opened by Queen Mary in 1922 includes a large entrance arch dedicated as a memorial to its employees who died in the Great War.

Among smaller railway stations in the suburbs, Gerald Horsley's Harrow and Pinner stations of 1912 must be mentioned as outstanding examples of just how attractive the free Neo-Georgian style could be in the hands of an Arts and Crafts exponent.

The other London terminus which was rebuilt during the early 1900s was Victoria. It was described by the same contemporary writer in 1901 as a 'station yard crowded with omnibuses, hansoms, four-wheelers, private carriages, vans and carts, as if to convince [foreigners arriving] of the energy and confusion of the London life. Not even an apology for a façade looks upon the yard'. But that indefatigable compiler of facts about London, H. P. Clunn, noted[9] that it was 'greatly enlarged in 1902–08 at a cost of £2 million and covers an area of 16 acres ... In 1907 the adjoining South Eastern station was refronted with a handsome new stone building in the Georgian style, which replaced the ugly wooden building that previously overlooked the Victoria Station courtyard'. This 'Georgian' façade of 1907–08 is in the very grandest manner of the time, with great Baroque caryatids and fruity detailing, though few people even today have time to look up at it in the continuing confusion of the station yard.

Fig. 68 Street entrance, Chalk Farm underground station, Adelaide Road, Hampstead (1905–07) by Leslie W. Green. A typical example, in ox-blood red glazed materials, of the numerous London tube stations of the Edwardian period.

Fig. 69   One of the first motor buses, running from London to Brighton each day, in 1905.

7 At Work – Factories and Offices

The end of the nineteenth century was a time of major changes in British industry and commerce, as well as in the employment of ordinary people, involving the formation of much of the country's economic framework for the next seventy years. Britain had become the largest industrial producer in the world during the seventy years following the Napoleonic Wars in 1815, but during the 1880s her annual production was overtaken by that of the United States of America. In 1900, the other giant industrial nation of the twentieth century, Russia, was far behind but was already showing startling economic growth after spreading her geographical boundaries the length of Asia during the previous fifty years. In Germany, in the late nineteenth century, rapid industrial growth was further accelerating with the growing nationalistic ambitions of the country.

Nevertheless, Britain was still the most formidable economic power in the world, particularly through her banking and foreign investment. Her industries, often first in their fields and so outdated by the 1880s, at last started to modernise in the 1890s with new products and the gradual adoption of electricity and oil. Her average growth of industrial production, an extraordinary 3·4 per cent a year during the half-century before 1870, was still 1·7 per cent during the years up to 1914 – nearly double the rate of population growth.[1] Cheap food from the developing countries of the world had ruined much of British agriculture, with the result that by the 1901 census, only 10 per cent of English working men were employed on the land compared with nearly 25 per cent in 1851. The rural population moved to the towns with much suffering, but with the possibility of better wages in industry or commerce. During the same fifty years, the numbers employed in textile manufacture increased very little, but those in the metal manufacturing industries, in building, in chemicals and in mining doubled, while the clothing industry (as against textiles) nearly doubled. Even more startlingly, the men employed in public administration and in the professions tripled, while the numbers working in commerce were multiplied by six and those in the railways by ten.[2]

Apart from the increase in railway employees, the most revealing aspect of these figures is the gradual trend away from rural labouring jobs towards industry and, for an increasing minority of people, out of industry into the type of clerical job which held the prospect of middle class status.

That is not to say that there was an end to poorly paid labouring jobs in London or other British cities. In the East End of London the poverty of the inhabitants was compounded by influxes of jobless farm workers from other parts of England and foreign refugees. The clothing manufacture industry, with countless sweat-shops and individual out-workers in the homes of the East End, was notorious for low

Fig. 70   At work in a factory in the late 1890s. The Lamson Paragon Supply Co. Ltd factory at Canning Town in the East End of London.

wages.[3] By 1911, 145 out of every thousand employed women and girls were making clothes, while many more were in other badly paid jobs – a lot of them were shop-girls, and the figure for women and girls in personal service as maids and cooks was still as high as 386 per thousand employed.[4] For working class men in the East End there was, apart from the factories, the possibility of manual labouring jobs of various kinds – from roadworks to the numerous big breweries – or of work in the great chain of London Docks. In 1900 the Port of London was the largest port in the world, handling much of an industrial export production only recently overtaken by the U.S.A. and imports of foods and other goods on an increasing scale which alarmed contemporary economic commentators.

Most of the London docks (like the big produce markets of Covent Garden and Smithfield and others) were built during the first three-quarters of the nineteenth century, although the Greenland Dock was opened as late as 1904 on the Surrey side, with disastrous financial consequences, for business was moving down-river. The major change in the docks of the years leading up to 1900 was their enclosure for security against thieves and the construction of large warehouses, many of which have been demolished or converted into flats as working dockland moved down-stream beyond Tilbury during the 1960s. In 1900 the London docks were still thronged with vessels, many of them sailing ships.

Lightness of hull, masts and yards, and a multiplicity of these latter, are the leading impressions conveyed to a non-nautical person by a modern sailing-ship. Steamers are seldom in evidence in the smaller docks ... The vessels seem to be crowded together in disorder but in reality they are systematically arranged ... Further down the river are the West India, the Millwall and the East India Docks, in each of which steamers of large

Fig. 71   Tallying wool bales, London Docks, 1900.

tonnage outnumber the (sailing) ships, until at the Victoria and Albert Docks and the Tilbury Docks ... it is rare to come across anything not propelled by steam ... Wooden ships have all but vanished. They represent an infinitesimal fraction of the total number of vessels built in the British Empire; the rest being made chiefly of steel. The employing of sailing-ships is rapidly declining–Lloyd's returns for last year [1900] indicate that in the period July–September no fewer than 171 steamers were launched, but only 6 sailers.[5]

For the dockers, life was hard when they were in work. They were poorly paid and had no job security. A dockers' strike at the West India Dock in 1872, for an increase from 4d. to 6d. an hour, spread to other docks and the employers were forced to settle at 5d. an hour. But the trading and cargo depression of the middle 1880s led the dock-owners to save money by the extreme application of casual labour by the hour, causing much hardship among the working men and leading to the famous Dock Strike of 1889. The dockers' Trades Unions, starting to feel their strength under the leadership of Ben Tillett and John Burns, demanded 6d. an hour and a minimum of half a day per engagement. With public support in hard cash, and with a dramatic intervention by Cardinal Manning,[6] the dockers won most of their demands after a four-week strike.

Relations between dockers and employers continued to be troubled and, with diminishing profits, the customers' facilities in the docks were not modernised. Widespread complaints led to the appointment of a Royal Commission on the Docks in 1900, which recommended the creation of the Port of London Authority. The government finally acted on this proposal in an Act of 1908 and the P.L.A. came into existence during the following year, with responsibility for operating the docks and charged with a duty to 'diminish the evils of casual employment'. Despite a pay

Fig. 72   The Schweppes soft drinks factory, Hendon (1896).

increase following a further dockers' strike in 1911, it was to take many years of gradual negotiation before the P.L.A. could be persuaded by the dockers' union to discharge that duty.

The dockers were by no means the only working men to organise unions at this time, for the Edwardian period saw the birth of trades unions' power in Britain. Rising prices and rising employment figures, combined with a very slow rise in working-class wages, were particularly favourable to their growth after the *Trades Dispute Act* of 1906. The total membership of all unions grew from less than two million people in 1905 to four million in 1913.[7] By that time the first national miners' strike of 1912 had given notice that Britain's working life had entered a radically different era.

Trades unionism was gradually to benefit many of the badly paid working classes, for it operated most easily against large employers, and this was a time when the trend away from the typical small business enterprise of Victorian times towards larger company units was becoming rapidly established. For employees of small industries and for clerical workers, increases of pay were much harder to obtain, despite the rise in the cost of ordinary goods in the shops becoming noticeable after 1906.

The widespread concern for public health and the Public Health Acts, however, did lead to some improvements in factory and office working conditions. Factories built at the time were more hygienic, better ventilated and had better daylighting than those put up in the nineteenth century. The new building techniques, with frames of steel and later reinforced concrete, were quickly taken up by factory owners; not only were they cheaper in many cases, but the frame left larger areas of floor free for work and of wall for windows than had load-bearing walls. Few industrialists building factories felt the need for the grand decorated façades or expensive materials wanted for impressive commercial offices, so simple elevation designs and labour-saving materials such as glazed bricks were popular.

A talented architect could do much with such a brief, as was shown by C. F. A. Voysey in his Sanderson's Wallpaper Factory built in Barley Mow Passage off Turnham Green in western London in 1902–03. Voysey treated the structural uprights as tall, elegant piers rising to the skyline. The absolute simplicity of the design is relieved by the shallow arches above the broad windows between the piers and by the delicately waving skyline above. With these, and very few other touches of decoration, Voysey made a straightforward block of white glazed brick into a work of architecture with great charm. There are few other factories of the time which show so much distinction.

In the prosperous West End of London the years immediately around 1900 are typified by a particular form of small office buildings, often with a shop below – it was later in the Edwardian decade that big company headquarters and office blocks for letting started to appear in large numbers. The tripling of the numbers employed in the professions (law, accountancy and the like), and the sextupling of those in commerce, during the preceding fifty years have already been noted. It was these types of business which occupied the new individual office buildings which appeared in the streets north and south of Holborn and Oxford Street.

Working conditions were extremely harsh for the clerks employed by such firms. Those whom improved schooling had enabled to rise to clerical desks from working-class family backgrounds must sometimes have questioned how much they had gained. A young male clerk might start a job at £50 a year, rising to £100 a year when he was aged about thirty during the Edwardian decade, while a rented two-bedroom

Fig. 73 Sanderson Wallpaper Factory (now Alliance Assurance offices), Barley Mow Passage, Turnham Green, Chiswick (1902–03) by C. F. A. Voysey.

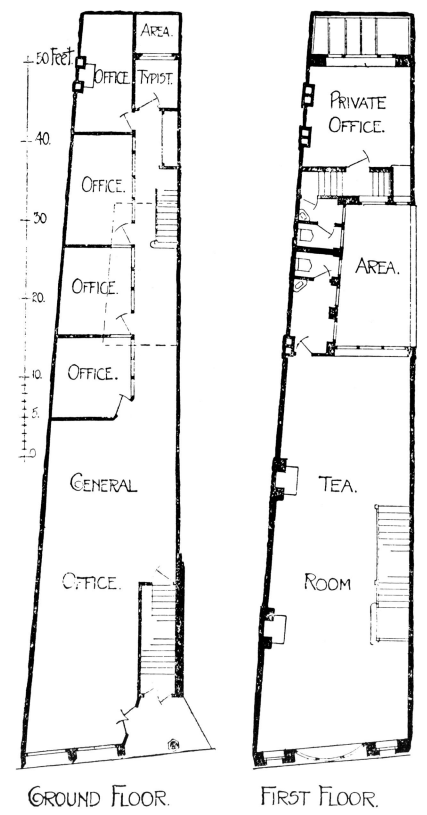

GROUND FLOOR.   FIRST FLOOR.

Fig. 74 Typical plans of a small Edwardian office building, showing the long narrow sites often presented to architects. By Trobe and Weston, *c.*1905.

house in the suburbs would cost him over £20 a year, with rates and gas and electricity coming to another £15 or £20.[8] Working hours were long, with only Sunday a free day. Office fittings often depended more on how prosperous the management wished to appear than on the comfort of the clerks. Since the building sites for such small office buildings were often long and narrow, with only a short street frontage, there was little daylight in most of the working rooms.

It is the street elevations which are the chief attractions of most of such buildings, north and south of Oxford Street, dating from about 1900. Today, most of their original ground-floor shop-fronts have been reconstructed many times, but the upper parts of the façades remain, inventive, often wayward but among the most attractive street architecture in London. Some architects made a particular speciality of these office buildings. Beresford Pite built the well-known No. 82 Mortimer Street in 1896, with his favourite Michelangelesque figures (carved by Slater) seated on either side

Fig. 75   House containing offices, No. 37 Harley Street, Marylebone, (1899) by A. Beresford Pite.
Fig. 76   Detail, No. 37 Harley Street, Marylebone (1899) by A. Beresford Pite.

Fig. 77   Offices and shop building, No. 3 Soho Square (1903) by R. J. Worley.

of a broken pediment and carrying a higher pediment on their shoulders. Pite's No. 32 Old Bond Street (1898) uses similar motifs, while his No. 37 Harley Street (1899) is a successful corner composition which combines a free use of the Arts and Crafts Baroque style with some outstanding architectural sculpture.

Another architect whose work can be enjoyed both in Mayfair and in Soho was R. J. Worley. His remarkable office building at No. 3 Soho Square (1903) is decorated with relief carved trees on its high walls, a favourite Arts and Crafts motif symbolising a bond with nature, and contrasts a swelling two-storey bow window with upper storeys which curve back into the frontage. Further west, No. 27 New Bond Street is another Worley design of *c.*1903. Worley's No. 1 Old Compton Street, on the corner of Charing Cross Road, takes the current English Baroque revival to wild extremes, with densely rusticated blocked columns and windows which seem to make the stonework buzz against the shiny walls of green glazed brick. It dates from 1904. Just as striking, and rather more disciplined, is the office building for T. J. Boulting and Sons, designed by H. Fuller Clark, in Riding House Street, Marylebone in 1903. In the City of London this original approach to office design makes a rare appearance in Bolton House in Cullum Street, off Fenchurch Street, with a bright green and blue glazed tile frontage of 1907 by F. F. Selby.

Perhaps the most attractive of all these small office buildings with shops below, however, are those by Treadwell and Martin. Henry Treadwell and Leonard Martin formed their partnership in about 1890. Their designs were usually of great distinction (it would be interesting to know whether their occasional disappointing buildings were the output of one of the partners), but the absence of any notable public building in England among their commissions has prevented them from receiving recognition. As it was, they specialised in office buildings, restaurants and public houses in the West End of London – more of their work will be seen in the chapter on pubs in this book.

Among their many office buildings, No. 7 Hanover Street (*c.*1900), No. 74 New Bond Street (1906), No. 55 and No. 20 Conduit Street (both *c.*1906) and No. 12 Woodstock Street (1907) will give a good idea of the sheer flow of exuberance and originality in Treadwell and Martin designs in Mayfair. Sometimes they took off from a Baroque inspiration, more often from a Gothic or Jacobean source. Best of all this series of their office and shop buildings is No. 7 Dering Street (1906), just off Oxford Street, whose main ogee arch sweeps to a point over the shop-window level, supporting two Oriel windows and a gable in a composition of extraordinary fantasy.[9] As a group, these buildings represent a successful attempt to introduce a new light-hearted city architecture to central London, far removed from the restrained Georgian tradition and perhaps only comparable with the gaiety of the gabled houses of Amsterdam built around 1650.

It should be noted that these West End office buildings, with their joyous originality, were almost all designed for commercial developers or for small companies. Office headquarters for larger companies or prestigious institutions dated about 1900 were, it is clear, expected to have more dignity and traditional style – and the style adopted for most of them was the revived English Baroque manner developed by John Brydon and John Belcher during the early 1890s and made fashionable by many Town Halls and by Government Offices in Whitehall from 1897 onwards. It suddenly became the style of the British Empire in 1900, at least for official buildings, as will be seen in chapters sixteen and seventeen of this book. Understandably, large business companies soon took it up as a style that was sound and grand and associated with British prosperity–exactly the image sought by successful businesses.

Many architectural historians have regretted the failure of British architects to develop further the sort of Free Style seen in the small office building just examined, feeling that the success of the Baroque was a resignation from originality and honesty in architectural design. But the Baroque varieties of Classical architecture are in fact exceedingly favourable to originality in design and it had some ideological backbone, as we have seen in Sir Frank Elgood's lecture of 1898 quoted in chapter four.[10] It was seen as a *modern* architecture for its time, rooted in the truly English Baroque style of Hawksmoor, Vanbrugh and late Wren before the foreign Palladian ideas ruined its inventive vigour.

This Grand Manner, as adopted for prestige office buildings, offered a wide range of expression. The headquarters of the North-Eastern Railway Company, built by the architect Horace Field in 1905 at No. 4 Cowley Street, Westminster, uses a grand version of the Neo-Georgian domestic manner – indeed, the office building seems more like a fine private mansion than business premises. Edward Mountford's 1901 headquarters offices for Booth's the gin distillers in Cowcross Street, Clerkenwell and Frank Elgood's own rather poor 1906–08 design of Dewar House (for another

Fig. 78   Offices and shop building, No. 74 New Bond Street, Mayfair (1906) by Treadwell and Martin. One of many delightfully inventive designs by this firm of architects in the streets around Oxford Street and Bond Street.
Fig. 79   Offices and shop building, No. 12 Woodstock Street, off Oxford Street, Mayfair (1907) by Treadwell and Martin.

distillery company) in the Haymarket, are good examples of the style's freely Baroque varieties, while A. T. Bolton's London office for the Hamburg–Amerika shipping line of 1906–07 in Cockspur Street is at the wilder end of the range. Two notable Neo-Georgian office buildings, Nos. 2–10 Tavistock Street (1904) and No. 42 Kingsway (1906), should also be noted here, for they were the first London works of the great architect Sir Edwin Lutyens.

Non-commercial organisations felt free to indulge in even more original versions of Classical architecture in their national headquarters buildings. Thus the Law Society engaged the great Charles Holden, chief heir to the Free Style tradition developed by the Arts and Crafts movement, to do one of his early free Classical buildings for the Society's new Library Block of 1903–04 in Chancery Lane. Holden followed this with the even more original headquarters for the British Medical Association at No. 429 Strand in 1907–08. These two buildings are among the most impressive works in London of the early 1900s. Both adapt the fashionable Classical or Baroque idioms of their time, including Beresford Pite's absorption of Michelangelo's Mannerism, and transform them into an architecture of powerful masses and original detailing. The British Medical Association building, now

Fig. 80 Offices and shop building, No. 20 Conduit Street, Mayfair (1906) by Treadwell and Martin.
Fig. 81 Offices and shop building, No. 7 Dering Street, off Oxford Street, Mayfair (1906) by Treadwell and Martin.

Fig. 83   The first of Lutyens's London works, the Neo-Georgian style Country Life Building, Nos. 2–10 Tavistock Street, Covent Garden (1904) by Sir Edwin Lutyens, still Baroque in its detailing.
Fig. 82 (*Opposite page*)   The Neo-Georgian office building.
Headquarters of the North Eastern Railway Company, No. 4 Cowley Street, Westminster (1905) by Horace Field.

Rhodesia House, became something of a *cause célèbre* at the time. Not only did the campaigners for a purer Classicism in *The Architectural Review*[11] dub it 'The Ugly Style', but the sculpture by Jacob Epstein which Holden integrated into the design was castigated by puritans and press as allegedly obscene. Sadly, Epstein carved the sculpture with the grain of the stone in such a way that it was subject to rapid erosion and this makes it difficult to see today what all the fuss was about.

The more elegant sort of Classicism which the purist campaigners advocated from 1906 onwards is well shown by the office headquarters of the *Morning Post* newspaper built on the corner of the Strand and the Aldwych in 1906–07. The architects here were Mewès and Davis, who also designed the Ritz Hotel and the Royal Automobile Club. The *Morning Post* offices, now spoiled by the addition of crass attic storeys, held up a truly Parisian Classicism of delicate astylar rustication and Mansard roofs as an example to London architects of office blocks (see Figs. 5 and 87).

This refined example was rarely followed before 1910 and the typical Edwardian headquarters building in the West End was Baroque. The style was particularly

Fig. 84   Redland House, No. 42 Kingsway (1906) by Sir Edwin Lutyens.
Fig. 85   British Medical Association (now Rhodesia House), No. 429 Strand, (1907–08) by Charles Holden, with the controversial sculpture by Epstein. Photograph taken in 1908.

popular with the insurance companies which were enjoying a period of rapid growth at the time. Writing in 1905, the architect Paul Waterhouse remarked on 'the appearance in our streets of vast palaces dedicated to the business of the great corporations who make their money by relieving people of risk'.[12] The biggest of the insurance companies, the Prudential, employed that writer's father, the eminent Alfred Waterhouse, to design their enlarged headquarters (1899–1906) in Holborn in his favourite red-brick free Gothic manner. But Waterhouse was almost alone in ignoring the fashion of the time. The offices of 1898 at 54 Parliament Street (the southern end of Whitehall), designed by Alfred Williams, are far more representative. With its wilfully asymmetrical composition, rich texture and free use of Classical motifs, the design shows a commercial architect moving from the eclectic mixture of styles of the preceding years to a novel composition of the features of one style.

The *Life Assurance Companies Act* of 1870 and the *Married Women's Property Act* of 1882, giving legal guarantees to insurers and the right of husbands to insure their lives in favour of their wives, created a background in which insurance companies

Fig. 86   Evelyn House, No. 62 Oxford Street (1908–10) by Charles Holden. The ground-floor piers of the steel frame structure can be seen in this photograph of 1910, most of them clad in brickwork.

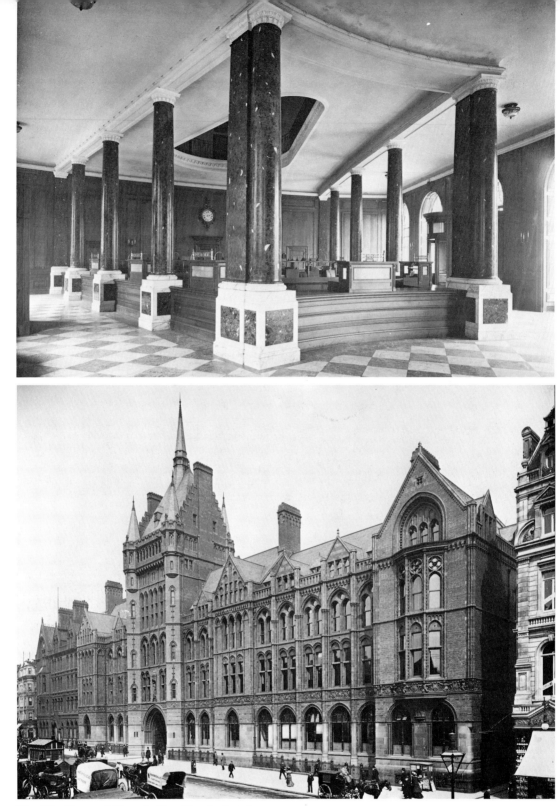

Fig. 87   The cool French Neo-Classical style.
General reception area, *Morning Post* newspaper, Inveresk House, Aldwych (1906–07) by Mewès and Davis.
Fig. 88   Prudential Assurance Company headquarters, Holborn, City (1899–1904) by Alfred Waterhouse.
Fig. 89   Royal London House (original part), Finsbury Square, north of Moorgate (1904–05) by John Belcher.

could flourish. But it was the tax relief for life assurances given by Finance Acts during the 1890s together with sales methods imported from the U.S.A. that led to the insurance boom and the building of those Baroque palaces of offices around 1900.

Evident prosperity would give insurance clients a feeling of solidity and soundness, it was felt, for their premiums would clearly be in safe hands. And so architects of grand public buildings were often commissioned by insurance companies, or else architects specialising in offices were called upon to excel themselves in grandeur. Public or limited competitions for insurance buildings were not uncommon, with famous architects invited to act as assessors.

John Belcher, architect of the Institute of Chartered Accountants in the City and of the Colchester Town Hall, was the designer of the new headquarters for the Royal London Insurance Company on the north-west corner of Finsbury Square in 1904–05, using the Baroque style closely associated with his name – an advertisement in an architectural magazine[13] at this time offered tutorial instruction in the Gothic, Renaissance, Classic or Belcher styles. The corner block of the building, with its broad curving forms and Michelangelesque sculpture, rises to a tower capped by the royal coat of arms which symbolises the central position which the insurance companies felt they occupied in the prosperity of the British people. The Alliance Assurance building at No. 88 St James's Street, St James's (1904–06) is a more controlled Baroque design by Norman Shaw in association with Ernest Newton.

The public interiors of these insurance offices were just as important a symbol of their wealth as their façades and no expense was too much. Thus in the general office at the entrance to the United Kingdom Provident Institution at No. 193 Strand (1902–06, now destroyed), the walls and desktops were of marble, while a relief frieze typical of good sculptural work of the period ran around the hall. The architect was Henry Hare, best known for his public libraries, town halls and university buildings.

The grandest of all the Baroque insurance buildings in central London is the Pearl Assurance headquarters at Nos. 247–261 High Holborn. The first section was built in 1906–1912 under the architects Moncton and Newman (the block was not completed until much later), making the Pearl the last of the luxuriantly Baroque insurance palaces to be started. The stylistic and structural differences between this extravagant manner and that of only slightly later buildings is well demonstrated by the two insurance buildings at the top of St James's Street on the corner of Piccadilly. The Norwich Union building, on the eastern corner, dates from 1905–07 and was designed by Ernest Runtz, one of those architects who often turned the Baroque style into a gross and self-indulgent affair. On the other corner, the former Royal Insurance building of 1907–08, is a very different matter. This is again by John Belcher, but here with his partner John James Joass, who did all the firm's design work from this time onwards. The building is one of the early steel-frame structures in central London, following the nearby Ritz Hotel of 1903–06, and the architectural expression is the outcome of that fact. An inventive Classicism and luxurious

Fig. 90   The Pearl Assurance building, Nos. 247–261 High Holborn, (1906–12) by Moncton and Newman. The last and largest of the High Baroque insurance palaces.
Fig. 91   Henry Hare: the general office interior, United Kingdom Provident Institution building, 193 The Strand, Westminster (1902–06). Demolished. Bronze frieze by F. Lynn Jenkins.
Fig. 92   Norman Shaw and Ernest Newton: Alliance Assurance building, 88 St James's Street, Westminster (1904–06).
Fig. 93   Royal Insurance building, western corner of Piccadilly and St James's Street, St James's (1907–08) by John Belcher and J. J. Joass.

Fig. 95   Main entrance, Electra House, Moorgate, City of London (1900–03) by John Belcher, with sculpture by George Frampton.
Fig. 94 (*Opposite page*)   Electra House, No. 84 Moorgate, City (1900–03) by John Belcher.

materials (the ground-floor columns here are of Pentelikon marble from Greece) were still *de rigueur* for insurance offices. But Joass used such features in an astonishing Neo-Mannerist fashion which, by emphasising the vertical thrust, makes it clear that the building does not rest on the load-bearing capacity of its stone walls and shows that the Classical details have no relevance to their traditional functions. This line of thought was to lead, a few years later, to the omission of almost all decoration in another headquarters office, that for the Kodak film company in Kingsway by Sir John Burnet and Thomas Tait, but few companies would have accepted such Spartan design before the Great War of 1914–18 (see Fig. 222).

Earlier in the decade, in 1900 itself, Belcher had started work on a major office building in the City of London, the banking and investment centre of the world. This building was Electra House, the headquarters of an international telegraph company, at No. 84 Moorgate. As originally designed, the building was encrusted with sculptural decoration of the Arts and Crafts type seen on the architect's earlier Institute of Chartered Accountants. But the design was changed and although the version built in 1900–03 (now the City of London College) includes some lovely sculpture by George Frampton around the doorway, the overall effect is of a rather heavy and ponderous Baroque.

Fig. 96   General office interior, Royal Insurance Company, No. 24 Lombard Street, City (1904). Interiors by Sir Arthur Blomfield and Son. Demolished and rebuilt 1910.

Belcher built a more striking work in the City in 1904–05, the new section of Winchester House in London Wall (destroyed 1960), with huge Atlas figures at second-floor level. Redevelopment was always happening in the City, but the major rebuilding was not to take place until after the 1914–18 War. The reasons for this were complicated. Despite England's world power and prosperity, increasing imports, together with the Boer War of 1899–1902 and the depression which followed it, led to uncertainty in the City's great financial institutions. There was even a cry for trade protectionism in 1903–06. Shipping and insurance offices, as well as various types of finance houses, were bringing great profits into London, but the uncertainty about the internal future of the country caused a massive increase in the investment of British capital abroad. In the Dominions and colonies of the Empire, and especially in the newly developing countries of South America, it was British capital which built many of the transport and other facilities necessary for their growth. As economic historians have pointed out, it is significant that the building industry in Britain was booming in the 1890s and up to 1905, while British capital investment overseas was low, but there was a building slump in 1906–10 when foreign investment became the dominant policy of the select group of men who controlled the City's financial currents.[14]

For most of the people who worked for these financial magnates and their satellite companies in 1900, working life was a matter of long commuting and long office hours in unpleasant surroundings. In the City, there were numerous

dens below ground in which ill-paid clerks worked for small firms under all-day artificial light. There were dusty garrets up four pairs of stairs in which six or seven people worked together. Light, in its narrow alleys, was so hard to come by that they tried to catch it by means of glasses projecting from each window ... Men worked underground and when they went out to lunch they again went underground ... On a summer day, one could look down through gratings and see clerks scribbling in books under electric light (which was just replacing gas) ... Wherever one looked the scene was colourless. The buildings had a tone peculiar to the City ... It was not so definite as the tone of mud or the tone of cobwebs or manure. It was such a tone as you might get from wet smoke mixed with Army-blanket fluff and engine smuts ... In some kinds of business the 'living-in' system was in force; the young clerks had a dormitory at the top of the building and a dining-room in the cellar; and, save for a few hours in the evening, they spent their young lives in that atmosphere. Nobody thought it anything but a sound system.[15]

The *County Councils Act* of 1888 had, like subsequent reforms of local government, left the City's self-government untrammelled and there was no political impetus to do anything about these working conditions for many years. There were major redevelopments at Finsbury Circus and King William Street, as well as Lloyds Avenue. Otherwise a handful of banking or other City institution buildings of the Edwardian period need to be noted here. Thomas Collcutt, architect of the Imperial Institute and the Savoy Hotel, built the Lloyd's Shipping Register offices, Fenchurch Street, in 1900–01 in a crowded but charming Arts and Crafts Baroque manner. The insurance offices at No. 1 Cornhill, with a dome over the City's main street crossing at the Bank, are by J. MacVicar Anderson and date from 1905.

Royal Exchange Buildings, in the broad passage behind the Royal Exchange, is a successful Baroque design of 1907–10 by Sir Ernest George and Yeates. The Scottish Provident Institution at the junction of Lombard Street and King William Street is a fairly distinguished Classical work with a giant order of 1908 by W. Curtis Green in the partnership of Dunn and Watson. This new restrained development in the designs of previously Baroque architects can again be seen in another insurance office, the

former Northern Insurance Building of 1906–07 at Nos. 1–5 Moorgate, one of the last works by the architect of the Old Bailey Criminal Courts, Edward Mountford. The great banks themselves are notably absent from the buildings mentioned[16]–their periods of sweeping demolition and new construction were to come in the 1920s and then again in the 1960s.

Fig. 97 Lloyd's Shipping Register, Fenchurch Street, City of London (1900–03) by Thomas Collcutt.

8 Shops and Department Stores

The giant department store in London is a phenomenon of the years immediately after the end of the century. A few smaller pioneers of the idea did open their doors earlier, but in 1900 almost all Londoners still used small shops which catered for people of all social classes.

The pattern of business in these little shops was very different from that in their present-day equivalents. Most shops, whether in the centre or in the suburbs, specialised in just one type of goods. 'When you went to the tobacconist, you found that he sold tobacco in various forms; nothing else. When you went to the sweet stuff shop, you went to buy sweets and that was all you could buy in that shop.'[1] Although bold display and advertising on shop fronts was common by the end of the nineteenth century, the interiors were normally dim and dull, relieved in slightly larger shops by the overhead cash-railway 'by which the assistant packed the bill and the money in a wooden ball and sent it up a spiral to an overhead track, whence it travelled across the shop and dropped off the rails into the cashier's desk ... dozens of balls whizzing along the rails from all parts of the shop ... and then making the return journey and dropping your change.'[2]

In the poorer residential areas around the centre of London in 1900, the outward display of middle-class areas was often missing. One writer described the streets in these poorer parts as follows.

> The shops are small and such as minister solely to the necessities of life; butchers who deal in cheap New Zealand mutton and inferior beef; fishmongers whose stock in trade is of uncertain age, with mussels and whelks and every kind of dried fish well to the fore; pork-butchers ... 'purveyors' of cow-heel and ox-cheek, of tripe and trotters ... fried fish shops. ... Should the back-street happen to have no regular shops, there is still business done. Numerous parlour-windows demonstrate the nature of the retail-trade carried on within; some by means of a couple of 'new-laid' eggs, as many loaves and samples of sweetstuff; others by a tailor's card ... the main characteristic throughout being that everything that can possibly be discoloured or mildewed is so ... Strong odours, compounded of boiled greens, fried onions, bloaters and toasted bacon, mingled with whiffs of old clothing, dustbins and family washing ... Dirty children sit and play on the doorsteps, share the gutter with the ducks and fowls or tear about the roadway, yelled at by frowsy mothers who, bare-armed and buttonless, stand at the doors and discuss local affairs with their neighbours ... These are not slums. They are simply the varying forms of the shabby, the seamy side of London.[3]

People did not habitually come from the suburbs to shop cheaply in Oxford Street at this time and the character of that street was much quieter than today. Regent Street and Bond Street, however, were already centres for jewellers and other shops selling luxury goods. The Regent Street of 1900 was still that of Nash's 1820s buildings – little remains of it today after the rebuilding of the 1920s. Bond Street, on

Fig. 98　Shopping in Battersea Rise, Wandsworth in 1904.

the other hand, was much rebuilt at the beginning of the century with a number of charming buildings on a fairly intimate scale. Of these, Beresford Pite's No. 32 Old Bond Street, Worley's No. 27 New Bond Street (*c.*1903) and Treadwell and Martin's No. 74 New Bond Street (1906), shop premises with offices above, have been mentioned in the previous chapter. But there are several others worthy of note,[4] especially two art dealer's galleries by Lanchester and Rickards at Nos. 144–146 New Bond Street (1911) and No. 14 Old Bond Street (1913).

Inside these fashionable West End shops, whether they were jewellers, barbers or bookshops, the fittings were notable for excellent materials and solid craftsmanship, rather than for any brilliance of design. A new flexibility of interior space was provided by the use of a steel-frame structure in such owner-commissioned shop buildings as Mappin and Webb's big jewellery store at Nos. 158–162 Oxford Street (1906–08, interiors now destroyed) and Mowbray's bookshop at No. 28 Margaret Street (1907–08). Both these shops were designed by J. J. Joass of Belcher and Joass and, as in his contemporary insurance offices in Piccadilly, their outstanding interest lies in the vigorous Neo-Mannerist style which he felt suitable for stone façades suspended on a steel frame.

Mappin House in Oxford Street was a large shop for its time, but it still specialised in only one commodity, jewellery. The department store was a very different matter, for it aimed to sell large quantities of almost all sorts of goods from sales counters

Fig. 99　Mowbray's Bookshop, No. 28 Margaret Street, off Upper Regent Street (1907–08) by John Belcher and J. J. Joass.

Fig. 100　Belcher and Joass: Mappin House, 158 Oxford Street, London (1906–08). The elevation consists of a taut skin of glass and Neo-Mannerist stonework, detailed by Joass, covering the steel frame structure of the building.

within one building. The idea was an American one and was being taken up at about the same time in Paris and Berlin.

According to H. P. Clunn,[5] it was William Whiteley who was 'the pioneer of the great London stores'. Whiteley had started a smallish department store in Queensway (then called Queen's Road) in Bayswater in about 1880. This store was burned down – Whiteley thought it was arson arranged by the local small shopkeepers – in 1887 and he moved his principal premises around the corner to Westbourne Grove, where his business proved a great success.

By 1900, other large shop-owners had decided to follow Whiteley's example. The first off the mark were Harrod's and the furnishing specialists Waring and Gillow. Harrods big department store in Brompton Road, Knightsbridge was built in 1901–05 and still remains one of the world-famous London shops. The building is in an old fashioned style for its date, designed by the otherwise little-known architects Stephens and Hunt (Stephens, Andrew Saint points out, was C. W. Stephens, architect of Claridges Hotel). Much of the detailing at Harrods is Baroque, but the overall manner is indeterminate rather than eclectic. It had, however, notable interiors such as the famous Meat Hall in a dashing Arts and Crafts style of tremendous charm. The use of pinkish-buff terracotta for the exterior, rather than stone, was unusual for a prestige building by that time. But these eccentricities have if anything reinforced the unique and rather snobbish symbolism attached to the

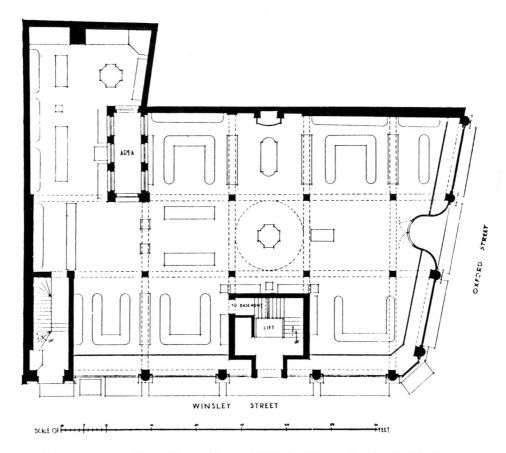

Fig. 101 Belcher and Joass: Plan, Mappin House, 158 Oxford Street, London (1906). The usable area provided inside the building by the new steel frame structure is in sharp contrast to the area occupied by older load-bearing walls.

Fig. 102   Interior, Mappin and Webb's Jewellery shop, Oxford Street (1908) by John Belcher and J. J. Joass. Interior now destroyed.

Fig. 103   Christmas poultry display in the Meat Hall, Harrods Department Store, Knightsbridge in 1901. The Arts and Crafts decoration has largely been replaced.

Fig. 104　Selfridges Department Store, Oxford Street, first section, 1907–09. Elevations designed by a young American architect, Francis Swales. Executed in consultation with Daniel Burnham of Chicago, supervised by R. Frank Atkinson. The building was later completed in stages until 1928 by Sir John Burnet.

name Harrods for the middle classes in Kensington and throughout the counties of England.

Waring and Gillow's furnishing department store at Nos. 164–182 Oxford Street was started at the same time as Harrods in 1901, but opened a year later after a dispute about Ancient Lights. The building was the first big commission of the Liverpool architect R. Frank Atkinson and the style he adopted was a swaggeringly Baroque development of Sir Christopher Wren's work at Hampton Court Palace, as specifically English a Classical style as any jingoistic patriot would ask for at the time of the Boer War. The interior was gutted and converted in 1977, but the main Atkinson façades have been preserved.

The next department store to open was Debenham and Freebody's in Wigmore Street, just north of Oxford Street, in 1909. The store was the London centre of a group of shops, in various parts of England, owned by Ernest Debenham, whose mansion in Addison Road designed by Halsey Ricardo was described in chapter five. When Debenham decided to rebuild and enlarge the premises in 1906, he did not commission his friend Ricardo for this work, for he was no specialist in the design of large buildings. Debenham turned to a talented designer, James Gibson – who had built three large town halls – but he did ask for a building in the glazed tiles which Ricardo had advocated for so long. The resulting Debenham store, now largely occupied by Hamley's sports shop, is one of the most characteristic products of the period, a large Baroque palace with a fantastic skyline–but its walls are entirely of glowing creamy Doulton tiles. So strongly have we come to associate glazed white tiles with hygienic bathrooms and hospital rooms, that it is still difficult to appreciate grand Classical columns and towers of that material. Gibson later built another department store called Arding and Hobbs in Battersea in 1910.

The same year that Debenhams opened, 1909, saw the opening of the first part of the most grandiose of all the London department stores. The owner, Gordon Selfridge, had been planning the gigantic Oxford Street store for some years before work started on the building in 1907. He wanted a magnificent stone-faced building in the American Neo-Classical tradition and the design of the façades was done by a young American architect called Francis Swales, who had studied at the Ecole des Beaux-Arts in Paris. All the same, Selfridge commissioned the eminent Chicago architect, Daniel Burnham, to be consultant for the design and it was Burnham's representative, Albert D. Miller, who designed the steel frame structure inside the building. The first part, built in 1907–09, was the eastern end of the Oxford Street frontage. It was erected under the supervision of R. Frank Atkinson (the architect of Waring and Gillow). After that, Selfridge commissioned Sir John Burnet, the great Scottish architect, to supervise the rest of the building in stages up to its completion in 1928. Burnet followed Swales's exterior design, but much of the detailing of the central entrance bay, with its idiosyncratic clock, and of such interiors as the lifts, show the Scotsman's unmistakable hand. Selfridges department store has a less class-conscious image than that of Harrods, but still fulfils a very important role in the lives of northern Londoners. Its broad internal spaces continue to function satisfactorily in all but the densest crowds seventy years after the first stage opened, an impressive achievement during a period of so much change.

Other department stores of a fairly specialised type opened in London during the pre-1914 period, notably Burberrys, the prettily Baroque clothing store of 1911–12 by Walter Cave in Haymarket, and the Heal's furniture department store in Tottenham

Fig. 105   Burberrys Clothing Department Store, Haymarket (1911–12) by Walter Cave.

Court Road, rebuilt in 1914–16 by Smith and Brewer in a new simplified style. But the last of the major Edwardian general department stores brings us back to the pioneer of the type, William Whiteley.

Whiteley's store in Westbourne Park had flourished so well since 1890 that he determined to have his own purpose-built palace. In 1908 he commissioned Belcher and Joass to design this for him on a site in Queensway where Whiteley had started business and the first part opened in 1911. Joass produced a long horizontal design for Whiteley which was just as remarkably Mannerist as his slightly earlier vertical steel-frame buildings had been. One of the visual principles of Classical, and even Baroque, design has always been that the lower walls must appear powerful enough to support the weight of the storeys above. The Whiteley design defies this principle, for the two-storey colonnade has a weight that appears to float above the broad street windows and narrow piers of the ground floor. Only a frame construction made this possible and Joass evidently wanted to emphasise that. Inside the store, the spaces use the freedom given by frame construction to great advantage, while the decoration has a delicate geometrical linear quality far from the Baroque curves of ten years earlier. The building was extended and completed by a northern end in an even less decorated manner in 1925.

The big Edwardian department stores changed many of the shopping patterns of London. Some people missed the old ways of the small shops, but most found advantages in the large stores.

> They are lighter, cleaner, brighter. The atmosphere is better. There is more space and more air to breathe. There is more display, or perhaps exhibitionism is the truer word. There is less servility and more actual service … there is a much more varied and fresher stock, and articles which formerly could be had only by the well-to-do are now available to the many.[6]

Their coming affected the lives of their workers as much as those of their customers, for the girls who had had no prospect of promotion in small shops now found better pay and some sort of a career structure among the big staffs of the stores.

The commercial success of the new department stores varied. Waring and Gillow, and Debenham and Freebody, have gone from their grand buildings. Burberrys and Heal's still flourish. Harrods and Selfridges have changed owners, but still retain their character and premises. Whiteley, who started it all in London, spent too much on his new building and sold out to Selfridge by 1930.

Fig. 106   Detail, Whiteley's Department Store, Queensway, Bayswater (1908–10) by J. J. Joass of Belcher and Joass.

ARTHUR GARRATT

9 West End Theatreland

The years around 1900 were one of the great periods of theatre building in London – most of the theatres in the West End still date from late Victorian and Edwardian times. This boom was not caused by a sudden increase in appreciation of dramatic art among London people. Indeed, J. B. Priestley has pointed out[1] that London impresarios largely ignored the great serious playwrights of the time – Chekov, Strindberg and Ibsen – and of the past, with the exception of Shakespeare. And, when such serious plays were put on, the audiences ignored them too. If plays with any thought-provoking content were to succeed, they had to be spiced with so much wit and humour – in the manner of George Bernard Shaw or Somerset Maugham – that most of the audience could ignore the underlying seriousness. Otherwise it was the light sentimentality of Barrie, the musical comedies and the naughty French farces which drew the big audiences; or, best of all, the music hall.

The reason for this attitude to plays, and indirectly for the style of the theatre buildings of the time, can be found in Londoners' attitudes to what they wanted from an evening at the theatre. Theatre was not an art form for most of them, nothing to do with education or the paintings to be seen in the new Tate Gallery. They went to the theatre for a jolly and rather grand evening out. Although suburban Londoners did not indulge in shopping expeditions in the West End until 1910, they did look to the West End for their celebrations and evening outings. At a time when more and more people were finding jobs that raised middle-class aspirations, the new theatres went up to provide them with escapist entertainment in grandiose settings.

Evening entertainment was not easy to find in the new outer suburbs, though there were thirty music halls in the inner suburbs.[2] The Dance Halls of the 1920s had not arrived yet. Dances were put on occasionally in the Assembly Rooms of many suburbs, at a charge ranging from threepence to five shillings, depending on the district. The *thé dansant* crept into hotels after 1910, and cinemas started to become common at about the same time. As we shall see in chapter eleven, eating out in restaurants was only just starting to become normal. For children too, there was little choice of outing. Circuses would visit some suburbs, and the Crystal Palace provided entertainment for those in the southern suburbs. Otherwise, there were the zoo, Madame Tussaud's waxworks and various shows such as Buffalo Bill's at Earl's Court or Maskelyne and Devant's conjuring displays in the Egyptian Hall in Piccadilly.[3] The Edwardian era was, of course, the high period of great international exhibitions – a new giant exhibition on a new theme opened every summer at White City, Earls Court, or later at Wembley. It was a time of growth for spectator sports too, with tennis, boxing and in particular football, attracting increasing crowds. But for most London people who could afford entertainments, an evening out in 1900 usually meant an outing to the West End.

Fig. 107 The Dress Circle of a London theatre, 1901.

Apart from the inner suburban music halls, there were fourteen others – usually the largest – in central London. Among the best-known were Dalys in Leicester Square and the London Pavilion in Piccadilly Circus, established there since 1885. The London Pavilion was reconstructed in 1899 and was hugely popular 'even in summer, when the sliding roof ensures coolness'.[4] More spectacular still were the

Fig. 108   The London Hippodrome, Charing Cross Road opened in 1900, by Frank Matcham.

new giant music hall theatres by the leading theatrical architect Frank Matcham which opened around 1900.

The first of these palatial music halls was the London Hippodrome in Charing Cross Road, rivalling the spectacle possible at the much older Drury Lane Theatre.

Fig. 109 Tower, Coliseum Theatre, St Martin's Lane (1903–04) by Frank Matcham. Matcham with his pupils Sprague and Crewe, dominated Edwardian theatre architecture. They used a wide variety of classical styles, of which the Coliseum is the best high Baroque example.

The Times newspaper reported on 1st January 1900 that,

> On Saturday next yet another new theatre will be opened in the West End of London; and a theatre which in purpose and design exhibits a wide departure from anything which has hitherto been attempted ... To a stage of unusually large dimensions has been added an arena, or circus-ring, capable of being converted by ingenious mechanical arrangements into a huge tank with a depth of eight feet and a cubic capacity of about 100 000 gallons. Thus in future it will be possible to witness in succession, without leaving one's seat, a theatrical performance, a circus and an aquatic entertainment ... The tiers of seats are concentric with the arena and are ranged in an unusually steep ascent ... The decoration of the building has been carried out on the most splendid scale in the Flemish Renaissance style and the effect is certainly very striking.[5]

The exterior of the London Hippodrome (the interior has been rebuilt), with its corner rib-crown topped by a chariot and careering horses, remains striking today. All the same, the design was done in about 1898 and its Flemish terracotta manner was already old fashioned among architects by then.

Matcham's next Music Hall cum Variety (called Vaudeville in America) extravaganza caught up with architectural fashion by using a flamboyant version of the English Baroque typical of the new public buildings going up at the time. This was the London Coliseum in St Martin's Lane, now used by the English National Opera. In March 1900 *The Builder* magazine reported that Matcham had obtained permission from the London County Council for a small theatre for 762 people on the site.[6] But as built in 1903–04 for the impresario Oswald Stoll, Matcham's design became a huge Baroque theatre seating over 3000 people. The programme for the opening on Christmas Eve 1904 announced that it combined 'the social advantages of the refined and elegant surroundings of a Club; the comfort and attractiveness of a Café, besides being the Theatre de Luxe of London and the pleasantest family resort imaginable'.[7] The Coliseum worked four variety performances a day to start with, but that was soon reduced to two. Spectacular events were performed on its 75 feet diameter revolving stage, which included three independent turntables within its expanse. Motor-cars and racehorses worked up to high speeds against the turn of the stage and these wonders were interspersed with turns by ballet dancers, acrobats and famous actors or singers. The great music hall stars of the time appeared there too, the famous Marie Lloyd, the dancing comedian Little Tich, Grock the clown, the elegant male impersonator Vesta Tilley and many others.

Meanwhile, another big variety theatre had opened on one of London's key sites, the western corner of the new Aldwych. This was the Gaiety Theatre of 1901–03. Ernest Runtz designed the interiors, but the theatre's chief glory was the Baroque façade designed by the great Norman Shaw when Runtz's first drawings were rejected. Sadly, the theatre was demolished in the 1950s (see Fig. 5).

Apart from the big variety palaces such as the Coliseum or the Gaiety, the typical straight theatres of about 1900 were much smaller, seating perhaps 1200 people in the rather crowded conditions of the time (later regulations have forced such theatres to reduce their seating capacities to about 800). Theatre design gained much from experience. Thus the talented architects Detmar Blow and Fernand Billerey produced a charming but poorly integrated design for the rebuilt Playhouse Theatre in Northumberland Avenue in 1906 (now a broadcasting studio), which compares unhappily in detail with the designs of the specialist theatre architects.

Fig. 110   Interior, the Queen's Theatre, Shaftesbury Avenue (1907) by W. G. R. Sprague, the most refined of the Edwardian theatre architects.

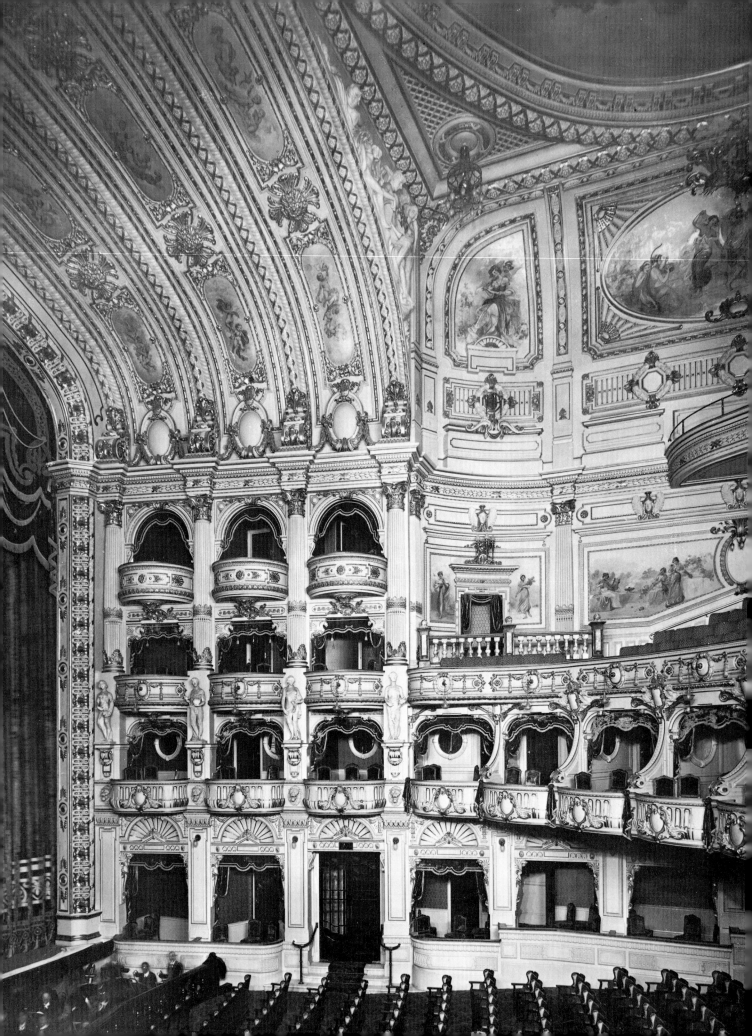

The architects who built most London theatres in the 1880s and early 1890s were Thomas Verity and C. J. Phipps. After Phipps's death in 1897, his mantle was assumed by Frank Matcham, but Matcham soon had to share the commissions of the time with two of his own pupils who started independent practices, W. G. R. Sprague and Bertie Crewe. These three designed and supervised the construction of almost all the lovely Edwardian theatres in London.[8]

The story of the splendid years of British theatre design in 1900 to 1910, and its sudden decline when the cinema became popular, is well told in Victor Glasstone's book *Victorian and Edwardian Theatres*.[9] It is Sprague who emerges as the most refined and distinguished designer of the three specialists in the field, although Matcham and Crewe had tremendous vigour and panache.

Just as old Thomas Verity's son Frank brought the French Beaux-Arts Classical manner to the design of mansion blocks, and Mewès and Davis to the design of hotels, at the time of Edward VII's Entente Cordiale, so Sprague followed the Baroque extravagances of about 1900 with a new Parisian refinement for theatre interiors. Between 1903 and 1907 Sprague completed the Albery, the Strand, the Aldwych, the Globe and the Queen's, each design inventively varied from its predecessor and each as efficient in operation and structure as it is elegant in decoration. The amount of

Fig. 112   The Stoll Theatre (originally Oscar Hammerstein's Opera House), Kingsway (1910–11) by Bertie Crewe. Demolished 1960.
Fig. 111 (*Opposite page*)   Interior, the Stoll Opera House, Kingsway (1910–11).

French influence varies – the Aldwych of 1905 has a particular Parisian flavour, the Globe is more English in its rich Neo-Georgian style, while the Queen's integrates Italian, French and English sources into a splendid amalgam.

Bertie Crewe was nearer to his master Matcham in feeling most at ease with giant spaces. In 1910, Oscar Hammerstein I decided to spread his entrepreneurial enterprises from New York, and determined to give the English capital a grand London Opera House which would outdo the Royal Opera at Covent Garden. Crewe's design for the Opera House in Kingsway of 1910–11, generally called the Stoll Theatre after the impresario who bought it when it failed within a year, certainly achieved Hammerstein's objectives in size and splendour. The magnificence of its proscenium arch, its arched sounding-board above the proscenium, its central dome and row of boxes beneath the circle (following a Viennese model) was beyond anything seen in London. The exterior, according to Victor Glasstone, was developed from Perrault's famous Louvre façade in Paris, but the general Grand Manner was typical of Edwardian England.

Crewe's Stoll Theatre was a financial failure because of its sheer size and perhaps its position, and its demolition in 1960 was a sad architectural loss. His other large central London theatre, the Shaftesbury (originally the Prince's) of 1910–11, has managed to survive after near destruction in 1970. The outside is a sorry jumble of

Fig. 114 Audience in the gallery of a music hall, *c.*1900.
Fig. 113 (*Opposite page*) The Shaftesbury Theatre (originally the Prince's), Shaftesbury Avenue, by Bertie Crewe (1910–11).

Baroque features, but the auditorium itself has the same formidable control of giant motifs, and integration of balconies with boxes and proscenium, as had the Stoll. After this, Crewe's Golders Green Hippodrome of 1913 is a disappointment, his timid interior trying unsuccessfully to come to terms with the purer Classical fashion of that time.

From the point of view of the history of drama, the most important events of these years took place away from the fine new theatres. In 1904 the Royal Academy of Dramatic Art was founded by Sir Herbert Beerbohm Tree. Slightly later, starting at the small Court Theatre (built 1871) at Sloane Square in Chelsea, Harley Granville-Barker ran seasons of plays by Bernard Shaw, Euripides, Maeterlinck, Galsworthy and others in 1907–09 which were to revitalise English theatrical production. But Sprague's new theatres witnessed the plays, and more particularly the actors, that kept theatrical life prosperous in the meantime. Star actresses of varying calibre from Ellen Terry to Mrs Patrick Campbell and the Royal favourite Lily Langtry kept the audiences coming to their performances and kept their colleagues well employed until the new cinemas caused the theatre to falter and then reorganise itself after 1912.

Fig. 115 The Victoria Palace Music Hall, Victoria Street, Westminster (1911) by Frank Matcham and Whitehead.

10 Publand

In London and other British cities, the year 1900 brought a dramatic end to the public house building boom of the 1890s, with hundreds of bankrupt publicans, and the rise of the Improved Public House. Pubs and the evils of alcohol played an exaggerated part in the ideas and statements of late Victorian social evangelists, religious and secular. The image of the poor working man drinking away all his weekly wages on a Friday night, leaving his family penniless, was widely promoted, and so excessive drinking, a symptom of social ills, was seen by many reformers as a main cause of those ills.

The pubs, with their gleaming street lanterns, bright lights and – in the larger ones – Music Hall entertainments, were indeed the only centres for enjoyment in the miles of London slums. Arthur Shadwell gave a picture[1] of such a pub in 1895.

This is one of the roughest houses in a very rough neighbourhood, but no fault can be found with the management ... The customers are equally quiet. They number about fifty and are scattered along the bar in the different compartments, some sitting down, more standing up, smoking and talking quietly ... What are they drinking? At the superior end some Scotch whiskies may be seen, a young sailor orders a rum hot, and a woman of the pavement at my elbow asks for a two of gin cold. But for the rest it is all beer. Several kinds of beer are sold at these houses, but the working-man confines himself mainly to the two cheapest, which are technically called 'beer' and 'ale'. The former is a very dark opaque liquid of the same colour as porter, but much weaker, and it costs 3d. the pot (i.e. quart) or 1d. the glass. 'Ale', otherwise called 'Four-ale' or 'Mild', is clear but rather dark in colour, and costs 4d. the pot or 1d. the glass ...

Two workmen come in perfectly sober, and one of them stands treat for two glasses of ale. His mate is in the act of drinking when the door opens, and two terrible-looking women rush in. The older is a wretched hag, who has already 'had a drop'. The other, a big heavily-built woman, is perfectly sober and in deadly, tragic earnest ...

'You've left me and the children to starve – me and the four bits of children. Ay', she continued, raising her voice and shouting at him for everyone to hear, 'you had two pounds on Friday, and what did you bring home for me and the children? Not one farthing ... And when you come home drunk and I rummaged in your pockets like a thief, what did I find? Seven and threepence. Two pounds on Friday night and spent it all but seven and threepence among thee – ye scoundrel!' She drags him to the door, thrusts him through, and as he disappears bangs him heavily between the shoulders.

Despite the concern about the effects of pubs, the demand from the public was increasing in about 1890 and both brewery companies and publicans over-reacted to it. Mark Girouard, in his fine study *Victorian Pubs*,[2] gives an evocative description of a dark autumn evening in the London streets.

Fig. 116 Delivery of beer in the late 1890s. Note the immense pub gas lanterns which often provided the only bright street lighting in poor parts of London.

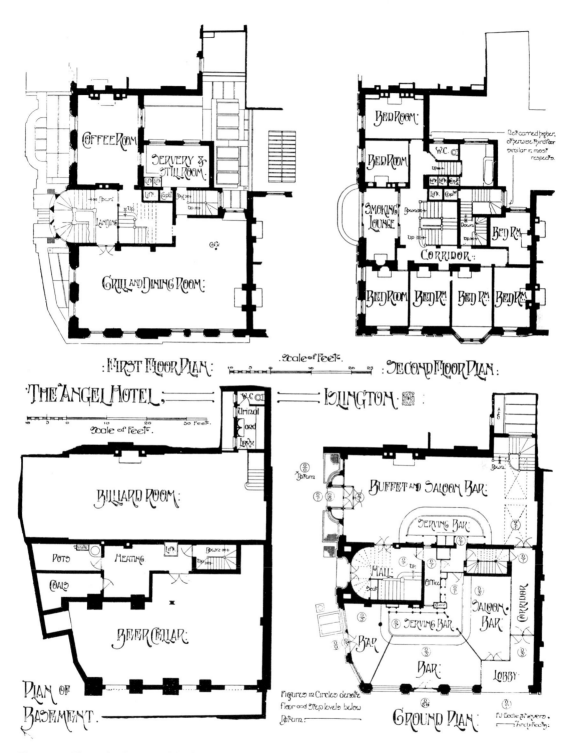

Fig. 118   Plan of a large public house of *c*.1900, the Angel, Islington, by F. J. Eedle and Meyers.
Fig. 117 (*Opposite page*)   The bar in the Dover Castle public house, Westminster Bridge Road, Westminster (1896) by Treadwell and Martin.

About seven o'clock, when the western sky was still red, the roads jammed with horse-buses, carts, traps and cabs, the horses' breath smoking on the frosty air, and the sidewalks equally jammed with a silent moving throng of people. A great proportion of London's working population still walked to and from work, often several miles a day. To solace them on their long and cold journey home, main thoroughfares like Bishopsgate, Shoreditch and the Mile End, Bethnal Green, Tottenham Court and the Old Kent roads were studded and in places crowded with pubs. As the street lights dimly lit up in the twilight, the pubs lit up far more brightly; long rows of monstrous lanterns stretched out into the street ... Innumerable glass-paned doors swung open and shut to reveal the warmth and glitter inside.

The glitter was certainly an essential part of the pub's attraction. In the hundreds of new or rebuilt houses that went up between 1890 and 1899, there were gleaming woodwork bars and back fittings, colourful plasterwork ceilings, large decorated panes of frosted or coloured glass and mirror. Large open fires with tremendous mahogany overmantels were usual, and many pubs built sumptuous billiard rooms in their upper floors. The style of these mahogany fittings was almost always a full-blown and extravagant Victorian Classical manner of unpredictably varied detailing. Gothic pubs were almost unknown, but in the late 1890s the novel decorative style developed by the Arts and Crafts movement was used in some interiors.

Fig. 120 Billiard Room of the Rising Sun public house, Tottenham Court Road (1897) by Treadwell and Martin.
Fig. 119 (*Opposite page*) Treadwell and Martin: the Rising Sun public house, 46 Tottenham Court Road (1897).

Fig. 121   Treadwell and Martin: the Old Shades public house, Whitehall, Westminster (1898).

The lay-out of the bars in public houses changed much during the nineteenth century. The first big gin palaces of the 1830s often had just one large ground floor bar, while the 'first-class tavern' of the next forty years would have a small public bar in the front and larger bar parlours secluded behind. In the early 1880s the fashion changed and pubs were built or rebuilt with a lot of very small bars – the Dun Cow public house of 1887 in the Old Kent Road, for example, had eleven bars in a tiny area. The island bar, in the middle of a pub's main room, was rare until the 1890s. Then it suddenly became all the rage and many of the host of pubs built during that decade had that arrangement – the survivors often retain it to this day, for it centralises the serving work and the space around the counters can easily be divided by partitions according to the changing fashions for bars over the years.

The exteriors of the new pubs were more concerned with eye-catching show than with pure style or other refined architectural notions. During the 1890s when an eclectic mixture of historical styles was used for almost all large buildings, the specialist pub architects (such as Saville and Martin, who worked for the empire of over fifty pubs owned by the tycoon Baker Brothers, William and Richard) adapted the designs of famous architects such as Sir Ernest George or Norman Shaw to produce flamboyant brick and terracotta houses with towers and high gables.

Late in the 1890s another firm of architects, Henry Treadwell and Leonard Martin, brought real originality and distinction to public house architecture. Treadwell and Martin's Dover Castle of 1894–95 in Westminster Bridge Road was a fairly typical London pub exterior of the time, as was the Leicester (now demolished) of the same date in Leicester Square. But their Rising Sun (1897) in Tottenham Court Road and their Old Shades (1898) in Whitehall have exceptional inventive delicacy in an Arts and Crafts manner based on the Gothic style. These two pubs, which are still in use with some of their original interiors, are comparable with the extraordinary series of office buildings which Treadwell and Martin designed around Bond Street during the next few years.

The Old Shades opened just before the crash of 1899. The causes of the slump were

Fig. 122   Detail, the Black Friar, Queen Victoria Street, City (*c.*1903) by H. Fuller Clark.

fairly complicated. The big breweries had competed hectically during the 1890s, encouraging their public house landlords to rebuild to draw the customers and often lending them large sums of money to do so. Mark Girouard has traced[3] a strange connection between alcohol consumption and the political party in power during this period. The consumption of beer and spirits rose when the Conservatives came

Fig. 123   The saloon bar, the Black Lion public house, East Ham (1908).

back to power in 1886–92, dropped under the Liberal government of 1892–95, and rose to new heights in 1899 after the Conservative victory of 1895. But the publicans all over the country had overspent on their grand new premises, and when a slump in beer and spirit consumption followed the outbreak of the Boer War in 1899, financial disaster for the trade followed. Publicans could not make any interest payments on the loans they had raised to finance their new building works. Nor could they sell out without a huge loss. A Southwark pub sold in 1897 for £33 000, changed hands again in June 1899 for £12 000.[4] Bankruptcies of pub-owners started to increase, first of individual landlords, then of the large groups. In December 1900 Baker Brothers themselves failed. Their liabilities amounted to £650 000, and many others followed as the brewery companies, who had been holding back their claims in the hope of weathering the drought, foreclosed. In 1898 the magazine *The Builder* listed eighty-four building contracts for new pubs. In 1900 it listed eight.

Out of the financial chaos that followed in the public house trade, a new movement arose. Old associations to encourage the 'improved public house' flourished as never before. Acting on the principle that Londoners could not be weaned from alcohol, but could be cured of excess, these groups aimed to convert the pub 'from a mere drinking bar into a well-conducted club.'[5] Meals, the availability of soft drinks and the presence of wives with their husbands were encouraged. Such groups had active support from peers and bishops, and access to capital to realise their aims. The most successful of them had bought up 114 pubs from ruined publicans by 1903, with another 200 due to come into its hands when their current leases expired. This organisation, the Central Public House Trust Association, developed into the countrywide company Trust Houses Ltd., now Trust Houses Forte.

Pub building in London did not cease entirely after 1899, but the style of the pubs which were built changed. The most famous pub of that period is the Black Friar in Queen Victoria Street, near Blackfriars Bridge. Its interior was remodelled in about 1903 by H. Fuller Clark, using the same coloured mosaic as he used in his Boulting and Sons office building in Riding House Street. But here he worked in freely Baroque forms, with arches of marble and swaggering decorative sculpture of the friars of the pub's name. This sculpture was by Henry Poole, a member of the Art Workers' Guild, and the whole interior can be interpreted as a jovial work of the Arts and Crafts movement.[6]

Some other pubs of the 1900s followed a simpler Arts and Crafts manner, with white roughcast and multiple gables, or with the Tudor timbering and inglenooks associated with Baillie Scott. This half-timbered style was to share the pub building market for the next three decades with the quieter Neo-Georgian style adopted increasingly by Arts and Crafts architects for domestic and other work after 1905.

Robert Thorne has pointed out that the pub slump of 1900 applied only to inner London. In the suburbs pubs were being built all through the Edwardian period – for example the brewing company Fullers in Chiswick built many after 1900, usually to the excellent designs of the architect Nowell Parr.

The brewing industry found it difficult to recover from the events of 1899–1900. The big companies had raised a great deal of new capital on the Stock Exchange to finance the pub boom of the 1890s and most of the shareholders who had subscribed lost their investments. Watney and Ind Coope paid no dividends in 1901, and many brewers wrote down the value of their share capital during the next few years by millions of pounds. Ind Coope were actually in the receiver's hands for a time in 1909.[7] But Londoners went on drinking and in time the brewing and pub world found a new stability.

11 Eating Out – Restaurants, Hotels and Clubs

The end of the Victorian and the greater part of the Edwardian eras (from 1901 to 1910) was an enjoyable period for eating out in London, except for the poorest classes. And it was not necessarily too expensive.

> Often and often, a friend and myself have met at six o'clock, possessing a sovereign each. We have had aperitifs. We have dined in Soho ... five courses, including game, and very good, though not Lucullan. We have had a bottle, often a bottle and a half, of reasonable claret, or flasks of Chianti, and have finished dinner with a liqueur. We have taken a cab to a theatre. We have bought seats in the dress-circle. We have taken a cab from the theatre to the station. At the station we have had a parting drink or so. And always even if we had gone to a Caruso and Melba night at Covent Garden (gallery 2s. 6d.) we got home with some loose change.[1]

The amount of food eaten by well-off people was extraordinary by the standards of three-quarters of a century later. Five courses was a reasonable dinner for a young middle-class man of some private income – for the wealthy, at grand restaurants and country house weekend parties, eight or more courses at luncheon and a dozen courses at dinner were common enough. Food in general was remarkably, almost artificially, cheap, for it was imported in vast quantities through the Port of London and its great food markets from the developing countries of the British Empire and elsewhere. These food imports had not only ruined the more expensive British agricultural industry – they caused much worry about the country's dependence on foreign lands to feed the forty-one million inhabitants of the British Isles, of whom six million lived in London.

> In 1800 ... if harvests were good, there was no necessity for importations on anything like a large scale ... how things have changed since then, and how utterly dependent the Empire's capital is in 1901 upon other countries for its food ... the eggs consumed in England in one year, one-third only being British, would fill 40 000 railway trucks ... in 1900 we imported butter to the extent of 17 million lbs., cheese $5\frac{1}{2}$ million lbs. ... the sums we pay away abroad in hard cash for what ought to be produced at home amount to millions sterling per annum.[2]

This writer's concern is no less genuine for his failure to recognise the hard economic facts of international trade.

The range of restaurants in London started to widen during the 1880s. At that time the grand restaurants and slightly less imposing supper-rooms of the West End were joined by middle-class dining-rooms – catering mostly for men – in the Strand, Covent Garden and the Haymarket. Families eating out together occasionally would almost certainly go to a nearby hotel. For many people, there was only the 'first-class tavern' and for the working classes nothing but their local 'cook-shop' or 'coffee-

Fig. 124   The kitchen in the Carlton Hotel in 1902.

shop'. About 1890 the tea-shop, catering for the first time for women unaccompanied by men, arrived and flourished. Soon afterwards the small restaurants, started during the 1880s by Italian, Greek and French immigrants for their compatriots in Soho and Charlotte Street, opened their doors to ordinary Londoners and the fashion for their more varied food spread quickly.

The tea-shop chain of Lyons and the inexpensive Italian restaurant chain of Gatti's grew rapidly before 1890, and Lyons started their teashop chain in 1894 and Cadby Hall food factory in west Kensington soon after the start of the century. The extension to a large popular restaurant, the Criterion in Piccadilly Circus (1899 by Spiers and Pond) can still be seen, although most interiors have been rebuilt.

Simpson's in the Strand (designed by Thomas Collcutt) and Rule's in Maiden Lane are rare survivors of the rather more expensive restaurants built during the 1890s and early 1900s. Romano's in the Strand, built in 1895 to the designs of the successful commercial architect Walter Emden, and Treadwell and Martin's magnificent Scott's of the same year in Coventry Street, have both gone. So have Collcutt's Holborn Restaurant, Carr's in the Aldwych (1902 by Goodall, Lamb and Heighway) and Beresford Pite's captivating mosaic frontage of 1903 for Pagani's in Great Portland Street; the lower storey of Pagani's was terracotta work in an eclectic late-Victorian manner by another architect, and Pite added three large arches with an expansive wall and cornice of bright mosaic-work above.

In 1904 the well-known Gaiety Restaurant moved from its old site on the north of the Aldwych (where Inveresk House now stands) to large new premises on the south side of Aldwych, the rear half of the imposing Gaiety Theatre. Like the theatre (1901–03) its interiors were by Ernest Runtz, its façades by Norman Shaw (who re-designed Runtz's original attempt). Its capacity was too large and it closed in 1908; by 1930 it had become the offices of the Marconi telegraph company.[3] This transformation saved that part of Shaw's fine Baroque design, which can still be seen, unlike the theatre which was demolished in 1955.

It will be noticed that only in the large Gaiety building designed in the high English Baroque years between 1897 and 1903 did current architectural fashion intrude into the special world of restaurant architecture. Otherwise, as among theatre architects with the exception of Matcham's loosely English Baroque Coliseum, the restaurant owners and architects sought exotic fantasies – usually with a Classical basis of sorts – that would stimulate customers who had those sort of expectations. Equally, diners with quieter tastes would seek the more restrained interiors of many Soho restaurants.

Fig. 125   Scott's Restaurant, Coventry Street, Piccadilly Circus (1892–94) by Treadwell and Martin. The restaurant has moved to other premises, but the building survives in mauled form.
Following pages
Fig. 126   Romano's Restaurant at Nos. 399–400 Strand (1895) by Walter Emden.
Fig. 127   Pagani's Restaurant, 42 Great Portland Street, Marylebone (1903) by A. Beresford Pite. The ground floor front already existed. Pite added the broad arches and the colourful mosaics above. Destroyed.
Fig. 128   The grill room, Gaiety Restaurant, Aldwych (1904), interiors by Ernest Runtz. The famous old restaurant moved into the building it shared with the Gaiety Theatre (all façades designed by Norman Shaw), but the new premises proved uneconomically large and it closed in 1908. The outer walls of the restaurant building survive as Marconi House.
Fig. 129   Tower Bridge Hotel (1897) by L. A. Withall.
Fig. 130   Drawing room in Claridge's Hotel, Mayfair in 1898. Sir Ernest George and Peto were the designers of the interiors of the hotel as rebuilt in 1895–99, while C. W. Stephens was the architect of the actual building.
Fig. 131   The Ritz Hotel, Piccadilly (1903–06) by Mewès and Davis.

By 1900 the really wealthy classes were increasingly turning to the big hotels when they ate out, especially to the new hotels whose luxury is still associated with the adjective Edwardian. In fact, new hotels of every type were appearing in many parts of London by this time, including sturdy bourgeois establishments such as the Tower Bridge Hotel (1897, by L. A. Withall) and the Norfolk Square Hotel (1897, by Treadwell and Martin). But it was of course the grand arrivals which made the biggest impression on central London. 'The total of the principal London hotels did not exceed a round dozen in the year 1855. In 1901 these figures, at a low estimate would have to be trebled, if not quadrupled. On every side are hotels large enough for palaces, gorgeously appointed and open to receive all comers with well-filled purses; while, in the Cecil, London possesses the biggest hotel on earth.'[4]

The Cecil, between the Strand and the river Embankment on the site of the present Shell-Mex House, was indeed exceptional. It was built in c.1890 to the designs of the commercial architects Archer and Green.[5] In a continuation of the quote above, the same writer continued, somewhat breathlessly, to extol its splendours.

> Throughout its interior many-coloured and costly marble and polished granite are used in profusion. Corridors are lined with hand-wrought tapestry and decorated in Pompeian style ... the passages are of the total length of 9000 feet ... it has a frontage of about 300 feet to the Thames Embankment and about the same to the Strand, while the four blocks of buildings encompass a central court and flower garden.

The Cecil is gone now – it was taken over as government offices on the outbreak of war in 1914, never reopened and was demolished in 1930. The Carlton Hotel in the Haymarket, whose interiors of 1900 were the first London work of the Paris-based firm of Mewès and Davis, has gone too, bombed in 1941 (the hotel itself, with the surviving Her Majesty's Theatre next door, was a slightly earlier design by the theatre architect C. J. Phipps). Another loss is the Imperial Hotel in Russell Square, built in 1900 by the Duke of Bedford's estate architect, C. Fitzroy Doll, in an eclectic Elizabethan manner with Art Nouveau touches. But its neighbour, the Russell Hotel of 1898–1900 (also by Fitzroy Doll) survives with its extraordinarily self-confident French Renaissance detailing carried out in terracotta.

The most sumptuous London hotels of the Edwardian period, however, are in one or other of the Classical styles. The style barrier was almost exactly 1900. The original part of the Savoy on the embankment was probably by Thomas Collcutt and built in a quiet version of his eclectic style in 1887–89. Claridges, the most exclusive Mayfair hotel, was rebuilt in Brook Street to designs in red brick by C. W. Stephens in 1895–99, with interiors by Sir Ernest George; again the style is mixed, as was the fashion of the time also to be seen in another famous hotel in Mayfair, the Connaught, designed by the hotel specialists Isaacs and Florence.

After the turn of the century, the Savoy was extended onto the Strand and here its twin cream-coloured blocks (which include the Savoy Theatre) by Collcutt are in a free but Classical manner, faced in the glazed terracotta made by Doultons.

Then came the three great stone-faced Edwardian grand hotels of the West End. The first and greatest of these was the Ritz, built in Piccadilly to Mewès and Davis's designs in 1903–06. It brought the French hotelier Ritz to London and the modern French Classical style with him. Its frontage in Piccadilly might well be lifted from a Paris street, and its internal planning has a clarity worthy of its Beaux-Arts trained

Fig. 132   Piccadilly Hotel, Piccadilly frontage (1905–08) by Norman Shaw.

Fig. 133   Ground floor plan of the Piccadilly Hotel, Piccadilly, the façades designed by Norman Shaw, interiors by William Woodward and Walter Emden, 1905–08.

Fig. 134   Second floor plan of the Piccadilly Hotel, Piccadilly.

Fig. 135 (*Opposite page*)   Restaurant in the Piccadilly Hotel (1905–08). Interiors by William Woodward and Walter Emden.

designers. The ground floor proceeds with logic, imaginative spatial transitions and brilliant decoration from the entrance in Arlington Street to the reception area (with the main staircase circling above it), on to the lounge called the Winter Garden and then to the great dining room overlooking Green Park. It was the first really large London building to employ a steel-frame structure (see chapter two).

Further along Piccadilly towards the Circus is the Piccadilly Hotel of 1905–08. While the interiors are the glory of the Ritz, it is the façades, on the entrance side and in Regent Street, which are the most memorable features of the Piccadilly Hotel. These elevations are by Norman Shaw (part of a scheme for the whole block, which was never completed) and show that the old master's inventiveness and sense of appropriate splendour were not at all diminished by age or the demands of the high Edwardian Baroque style. The interior of the hotel was planned and decorated by Woodward and Walter Emden and is pleasing enough, if an anti-climax after the tremendous frontages. The Piccadilly side was intended to have two of Shaw's towering gables, at either end of the screen of giant columns, but the hotel failed to obtain the land for the eastern side and only one gable was built.

The third of these Edwardian hotels is the Waldorf in the Aldwych, designed by A. G. R. Mackenzie for his father's architectural firm of A. Marshall Mackenzie and Son (a distinguished Scottish practice). The Waldorf of 1906–08 shows the adaptation of the splendid French hotel manner in a large-scale Classical frontage and luxurious interiors which include a big Palm Court. The Waldorf has survived with relatively

few internal reconstructions and could easily be restored to much of its full Edwardian splendour.

Many of the patrons of these luxury hotels were foreign visitors to London and the hotel building boom in most European capitals at this time was a sign of a reduction in the rentable accommodation available, coinciding with increasing travel by newly prosperous people of all the European and North American industrial countries. Many of the clients, especially in the hotel restaurants were British, for an increasing number of Londoners were moving up into higher income groups and could afford these or other expensive places in which to lunch and dine. Inevitably, the West End social clubs were another goal for such newly successful men and club membership increased considerably.

The old clubs, concentrated around St James's Street and Pall Mall absorbed as many new members as their social class awareness permitted, without increasing their premises greatly. Some interior refitting was carried out, for instance the new rooms done for the Grosvenor Club at No. 1a Dover Street in 1903. On the whole, the aristocratic and top professional members of the famous clubs were not likely clients for the large-scale approach of many Edwardian architects, for intimate scale and lack of show has always been a foible typical of long-established eminence in England. Here and there, one of the top social clubs did enlarge its premises. The Cavalry Club's extension at No. 127 Piccadilly (1908) is a good example of this

Fig. 136 Clubland for men 1903. The Morning Room, with its leather-upholstered chairs, of the Grosvenor Club at No. 1A Dover Street, Mayfair.
Fig. 137   United Universities Club, Pall Mall East, Westminster (1906–07) by Sir Reginald Blomfield.

unostentatious excellence, as well as a good quiet piece of Mewès and Davis design.

Two important new clubhouses were built in London during Edwardian times, both, rather ironically, in a French-influenced style. The first was for the United University Club, which decided to rebuild its premises in Pall Mall East in 1906–07. The architect commissioned was Sir Reginald Blomfield, the fierce leader of the current campaign for purer forms of Classicism and especially for the excellence of the French manner.[6] If Mewès and Davis brought the genuine French article to London in their architecture, Blomfield gave it the weight of his vigorous intellect and his position within the architectural establishment of the day. His United University Club building (its interiors are intact although it has been used as offices since the club left in about 1960) shows the taut but light rustication, spare use of the orders and Mansard roofs typical of the Parisian manner.

The needs of another class of would-be clubman were met in 1908–11 by the building of the Royal Automobile Club on the site of the old War Office further west in

Fig. 138   The palatial West End club of Edwardian times. The Royal Automobile Club, Pall Mall, St James's (1908–11) by Mewès and Davis.

Pall Mall. West End clubs traditionally brought together members with backgrounds or interests in common, and what could be more suitable for 1908 than that newly burgeoning group, the motorists? It gave entry to clubland to people who could never claim the social status, so important to most people at the time, which would secure membership of White's or even of the Reform further along Pall Mall from the R.A.C. site. The architects were Mewès and Davis, and again the style of the exterior was French – but a palace-type French rather than the *hôtel* or *hôtel de ville* manner of the Ritz. And it was a palace among clubs. The immense rooms, in a variety of styles (incorporating the War Office's Adam ceiling in the smoking room), included restaurants, a swimming pool, a big gallery for concerts and receptions, rackets courts and a gymnasium. It was quite different from the traditional neighbouring clubhouses of St James's, but it was the right large-scale venture for its period. By the 1920s it had a membership of 20 000[7] and, if by that time the status of 'motorist' meant little, the membership of a West End club still meant much.

Fig. 139   Mewès and Davis: entrance hall, Royal Automobile Club, Pall Mall, London (1908–11).

12 The Churches

Victorian England had been a scrupulously church-going society. The National Religious Census in 1851 revealed that forty per cent of the whole population, including infants and the aged, attended at least one church service on a Sunday. Not surprisingly, the rate was highest in rural areas, lowest in London. By the end of the century, church-going was declining rapidly. Local surveys showed thirty per cent church attendances in the countryside, and only twenty per cent in towns.[1]

The reason for this decline is suggested (though perhaps overstated) by George Bernard Shaw in his essay 'On going to Church' of 1896.

> There is still one serious obstacle to the use of churches on the very day when most people are best able and most disposed to visit them. I mean, of course, the services. When I was a little boy, I was compelled to go to church on Sunday; and though I escaped from that intolerable bondage ... to this day, my flesh creeps ... The mere nullity of the building could make no positive impression on me; but what could, and did, were the unnaturally motionless figures of the congregation in their Sunday clothes and bonnets, and their set faces, pale with the malignant rigidity produced by the suppression of all expression. And yet these people were always moving and watching each other by stealth, as convicts communicate with each other.[2]

After church, Sabbath observation was fierce in the home. Thomas Burke wrote

> The puritanical Sunday had little to do with things of the spirit. It was concerned with material things ... distractions from that quietude in which alone the spirit can grow ... One was taken to church *at least* once a day; and for the rest one could amuse oneself with the bound volumes of *Sunday at Home, Good Words* and *The Leisure Hour* ... anything amusing was barred ...[3]

As middle classes and working classes moved gradually towards financial and social freedoms, many of them dropped this previously almost obligatory practice.

Despite the drop in church-going, a general belief in Christian doctrine still formed the background to most people's lives. Church of England baptism of children was practised by two-thirds of parents at the start of the twentieth century, in addition to the other sectarian baptisms. Marriages took place in church. Sunday schools continued to flourish and establish Christian assumptions in children's minds, while the Boy Scout and Girl Guide movement offered an alternative which attracted increasing numbers during Edwardian times. Among adults, the period saw a trend away from the Church of England towards the Nonconformist sects, many of which were identified with particular social classes. Paul Thompson, the social historian, has pointed out that the Nonconformist recruitment from the prosperous middle classes was largely done by Wesleyan Methodists and Congregationalists,

Fig. 140   A wedding of ten young couples in a church at Walworth, South London, *c*.1900.

from the lower middle classes by the Baptists and from the working classes by Primitive Methodists and others. By the end of Edward VII's reign in 1910, there were more active Nonconformists than Anglicans in England.[4]

Despite all this, many new churches for the established Church of England, as well as for the Nonconformist sects, continued to be built. And their commonest architectural style was still basically the Gothic accepted as the proper Christian style for the preceding sixty years.

The range of Gothic types, however, widened considerably around 1900. Of the great mid-Victorian Gothic church architects, Pearson and Butterfield died right at the end of the nineteenth century, but Bodley worked for some years into the twentieth. This ageing master developed a new lightness of form in his late churches – a shift which can be seen in the work of other architects too. Their Gothic tended more towards roots in the last English medieval style, the Perpendicular, and even showed some new features which had no scholarly source in medieval work at all.

This tendency towards lightness and breadth was partly due to the introduction of new structural techniques such as the use of metal framed roofs popularised by Norman Shaw's famous 1880s church at Leek in Cheshire. But at the same time, architects such as George Gilbert Scott junior and the west country architect John Dando Sedding became increasingly interested in the Arts and Crafts movement. Scott was an experimental designer, while Sedding introduced quite novel forms of Gothic decoration unconnected with structural innovation in his last church

Fig. 141   Street railings (*c.*1891), Holy Trinity Church, Sloane Street, Chelsea, part of the furnishings by Henry Wilson for Sedding's church.

designs. In 1888 one of the most talented young Arts and Crafts architects, Henry Wilson, became Sedding's chief assistant and the designs coming from their office became even more original. This can best be seen in the Holy Trinity Church, Sloane Street, Chelsea of 1888–90, London's finest early Arts and Crafts church. The nave is broad and spacious, the tracery in the immense east and west windows flowing and inventive, the street frontage a strong composition anchored by four imposing turrets. The decoration and detail, which is of great beauty and originality, was mostly designed and carried out by Wilson and Ernest Gimson after Sedding's death in 1891.

Wilson's vigorous imagination can again be seen in his design of 1892 for St Peter's Church in Mount Park Road, Ealing in the western suburbs. This commission had been given to Sedding, but he left only a few notes on it at the time of his death, and the church is Wilson's design. Here the west window is made into a three-dimensional composition by recessing it under a deep arch, which is supported by slender free-standing buttresses. Wilson played strange games with the roof, too, bringing the interior piers of the nave up through the slates and linking the resulting turrets by shallow arches outside. Again, the tracery in the windows shows the freshness associated with the Gothic style as developed by Arts and Crafts designers. This decorative approach is seen in later London churches, such as St Luke's Church in Kidderpore Avenue, Hampstead, built in 1898 by the distinguished older architect, Basil Champneys.

Fig. 142 St Peter's Church, Mount Park Road, Ealing (1892) by Henry Wilson.

Relatively few new churches were built in central London at this time. Here the existing churches were often well attended, for it was the era of the Great Preachers.

People went then to hear Great Preachers as today they go to the Albert Hall to hear great singers ... they could be counted thickly. Spurgeon himself, Dr Parker, F. B. Meyer,

Fig. 143   Detail, St Luke's Church, Kidderpore Avenue, Hampstead (1898) by Basil Champneys.

Bernard Vaughan, Hugh Price Hughes and others ... how they were discussed and weighed and compared and how Aunts would come with news of a wonderful preacher heard ... Parties would then be made up to visit this new discovery, and on return they would sit about criticising his matter, his delivery, his gestures, and how far he surpassed or fell short of their particular standards of unction and oratory.[5]

Fig. 144   George Frampton, sculptor: a bronze memorial (1898). Frampton, later Sir George, was one of the best of several very fine sculptors of the period.

Within the Church of England, it was also a time of dispute about ritual. A campaign arose called the English Use movement, which urged a return to the simple church service ritual prescribed in the Prayer Book of 1549. It was this movement, which opposed church furnishings suggested by later accretions to the pure ritual, that led to the building of Sir Ninian Comper's first church in London. This is St Cyprian's, Clarence Gate – on the west side of Regents Park – built in 1901–03 'only to fulfil the ideal of the *English* Parish Church ... in the last manner of English architecture.'[6] By these words, Comper meant the Perpendicular Gothic, before the import of Renaissance features in Elizabethan times.

An even finer church, having arguably the best Edwardian church interior in

Fig. 145   Holy Trinity Church, Prince Consort Road, Kensington (main part 1902–04, completed later) by G. F. Bodley.
Fig. 146   Holy Trinity Church, Kingsway (1910–12) by John Belcher and J. J. Joass. One of the few churches in the Edwardian Baroque style. Joass designed a huge tower to be built above this frontage, but funds were never raised for this or for the internal decoration.

London, was started a year after St Cyprian's. This is the great Gothic architect G. F. Bodley's last London building, Holy Trinity Church, Prince Consort Road, Kensington, close to the Albert Hall. The first part was built in 1902–04, with high slender piers which rise to delicate pointed arches and a lightly vaulted timber ceiling. The church is little visited now, partly because its doors are too often locked, and partly because its quiet street frontage does not make the passer-by expect the soaring interior beauty.

The other important Anglican church of the Edwardian decade in the middle of London contrasts sharply with those already mentioned. Far from being in the traditional Gothic manner, Holy Trinity Church in Kingsway has a curvaceous

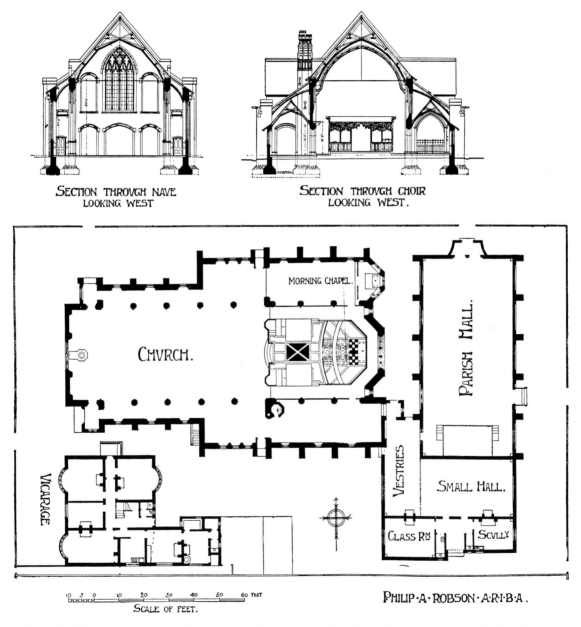

SECTION THROVGH NAVE LOOKING WEST

SECTION THROVGH CHOIR LOOKING WEST.

CHVRCH.

MORNING CHAPEL.

PARISH HALL.

VICARAGE

VESTRIES

SMALL HALL.

CLASS RM

SCVLLY

10 5 0 10 20 30 40 50 60 FEET
SCALE OF FEET.

PHILIP·A·ROBSON·A·R·I·B·A.

Fig. 147   Plan and sections of St Andrew's Church, Torridon Road, South London, by Philip Robson, c.1901.

Fig. 148   All Saints Church, Franciscan Road, Tooting (1905–06) by Temple Moore.

Fig. 149 St Jude's Church, Hampstead Garden Suburb (1909–13) by Sir Edwin Lutyens.

Baroque façade of Portland stone. This building dates from 1910–12 and it was designed by J. J. Joass of the Belcher and Joass partnership, which produced some of the best-known Baroque office buildings described elsewhere in this book. The style was of course chosen to harmonise with the other new buildings of Kingsway. The church was intended to have a tall tower above the frontage and the interior was to be decorated with Baroque plasterwork. Neither could be afforded, so the interior was left in its present impressive naked brickwork. In many ways, it seems curious that the church was built at all, for the construction of Kingsway had involved the removal of most of the surrounding inhabitants when the slum on the site was demolished.

Slums elsewhere in London were of course the centre of many church activities, but these efforts by religious and other charities will be described in the next chapter. As far as the use of churches themselves is concerned, contemporary clergymen often became despairing about the poor. The efforts to attract congregations were considerable. For example, St Dunstan's Church in Stepney had six working clergymen, nine scripture readers and visitors, and more than a hundred voluntary workers, with many social services attached. Yet Paul Thompson reports the verdict of the time, 'You can buy a congregation, but it melts away as soon as the payments cease.'[7]

The one area of London where the churches did find new congregations was in the suburbs, and that is where most Edwardian churches were built. When middle class people moved out of the grimy centre into the new respectable suburban milieu, churches were needed to act as centres for these communities of strangers. New buildings went up quickly, usually paid for by subscriptions raised among the newcomers. One instance was at Hadley Wood, where in 1911 an average of £15 per household was quickly subscribed for a church to be built.[8]

The slender piers and broad naves already noted in contemporary inner London churches were usually found in the new designs for the suburbs. This was not just a matter of artistic taste. The clergy now put less emphasis on the expression of mystery in the interiors, more on the visibility of the service for all present. A major instructional book of 1907 on building techniques and design[9] gives St Andrew's Church, Torridon Road, Catford by Philip A. Robson as a good example. 'The nave is of much greater width in proportion to the length of the church, while the aisles are narrowed till they become mere passageways ... As a result of this, there is hardly a seat in the whole house from which a clear view cannot be obtained of the wide open chancel.'

There are great numbers of excellent Edwardian churches in the outer suburbs of London and only a few can be mentioned individually here. St Michael Bassishaw, Hertford Road, Edmonton (1901) is a good instance of the work of that fine architect W. D. Caröe, who built other suburban churches such as St Barnabas at Walthamstow (1902), as well as the Church Commissioners' own offices of 1903 on Millbank.

In south London, All Saints' Church, Franciscan Road, Tooting (1905–06) is by the greatest of all Edwardian Gothic architects, the Yorkshire-born Temple Moore. Here, in a working-class suburb close to the London County Council's Totterdown Estate of cottages (see chapter three), Moore built a big church in a style which was perfected in his maturity. The building material is an uninspiring London brick. But the design shows Moore's exceptional mastery of glorious spaces around its wide nave inside, while the exterior is one of his best compositions of strong solid forms of varying sizes, rising to the tower. St Luke's at Eltham (1906) is also by Moore.

The other Church of England building which must be mentioned is one of Sir

Fig. 150   Entrance, Free Church, Hampstead Garden Suburb (1909–13) by Sir Edwin Lutyens.

Edwin Lutyen's most famous early London works. St Jude's Church soars from its hilltop site above the carefully planned spaces of Hampstead Garden Suburb. Built in 1909–13, the church shows Lutyens mixing a number of historical styles into one that is very much his own. The interior spaces are, as in Temple Moore's church, of rich imagination. Outside, the roof sweeps down from its ridge nearly to ground level, wrapping around the tower with its dramatic bell-stage voids and high spire.

There is another Lutyens church of the same vintage at Hampstead Garden Suburb. The Free Church, built to serve the Nonconformist residents, stands on the other side of the central green square from St Jude's. It is an intensely compact design in a freely Baroque manner, more earth-bound than the heaven-reaching heights of its Anglican neighbour. Such combined churches of Nonconformist sects were a feature of the Edwardian decade, for it was a time of many changes for most of them.

The identification of particular sects with various social classes has already been noted. But there was also something of a political link between Nonconformists and Liberals and between Anglicans and Conservatives. Thus a growth of Nonconformism preceded the Liberal victory in the General Election of 1906, while the swing to the Conservatives during the next few years was accompanied by a revival in the Church of England.

The character of Nonconformism was changing too. The hellfire fervour of chapel services in the mid-nineteenth century lost favour with most younger members of these churches from the 1890s onwards and a new humanitarian concern was emphasised – despite the outbreaks of religious hysteria that accompanied the upsurge of chapel-going in Wales in 1905.

Numerous Nonconformist churches and chapels were built in the Edwardian suburbs at the same time as the Anglican buildings already mentioned. The layout and basically Gothic style of most of these buildings differed little from contemporary work for the established Church, except that Baptist services placed emphasis on a central plan around the font for total immersion. But the various sects did develop likings for architectural styles which would express their difference from the conventional Gothic of Church of England buildings. Thus designs such as George Baines's Presbyterian (now the United Free) Church on the Broadway at Muswell Hill (1902) or James Gibson's Wesleyan Methodist Church in Upper Tooting (c.1904) show characteristic Arts and Crafts influence in their Gothic detailing and employ particular building materials – napped flint, terracotta and others – to achieve their own special effect. The Muswell Hill church, one of the most extreme of its kind, is also notable for its roof structure, an early example of the steel truss system developed by Messrs. Dawnay and Sons. Other good Nonconformist churches, among dozens in the suburbs, include the interesting United Free Church at Woodford Green in north-east London constructed in a vaguely Byzantine manner (1903–04 by C. Harrison Townsend), the Baptist Church at Cricklewood by Arthur Keen and a rather pretty Presbyterian Church in the Finchley Road at Golders Green (1910 by T. Phillips Figgis). Finally, among the Protestant sects of Christianity, in 1907 the Quakers built a delightful Friends' Meeting House in an Arts and Crafts manner reminiscent of Voysey at the top of Heath Street, Hampstead, designed by Fred Rowntree.

The other great branch of Christianity, the Roman Catholic Church, had been building London churches steadily ever since the British law permitted this at the beginning of Queen Victoria's reign. Now, at the end of the nineteenth century, the Catholics' vision of a cathedral in Westminster became real. It was an important symbol to that church, for there was still much anti-Catholic feeling – especially

Fig. 151   United Reformed Church, Broadway, Muswell Hill (1902–03) by George Baines.

among the English working classes, who identified Catholicism with the cheap Irish labour which they believed cost them their jobs.

In 1895 Cardinal Vaughan appointed John Francis Bentley, a convert and the designer of a number of earlier Catholic churches in the Gothic style, as architect for the cathedral. The site, just off Victoria Street, had already been purchased and Bentley went off on a visit to Italy with the Cardinal to look for inspiration. The decision was made to build a Byzantine cathedral, as this had been the earliest known style of the Roman Church. It was also significant that this would differentiate the building strongly from the Anglican Gothic tradition, as well as from the nearby Westminster Abbey.

In fact, Bentley's design makes no attempt at a scholarly revival of Byzantine architecture. Many of its motifs are derived from that style, while the plan has both the great dome-topped spaces and a development of the basilica form seen in various Byzantine churches, though rarely together. But numerous other features show the influence of the fashions of the 1890s, and the overall use of banded stone and brickwork is more typical of that time than any other.

If we look only at the style and detailing of Bentley's cathedral, however, we would miss the whole essence of one of the greatest buildings of its time. In the big architectural matters, the composition of the solid forms of the exterior and the breathtaking enclosure of vast spaces within, a visit to the cathedral offers one of the

Fig. 152   Design for the United Free Church, Woodford Green (1903–04) by C. Harrison Townsend. The exterior is shown as built, except that Townsend's Symbolist tower was never executed.

supreme experiences in London. When it opened to the public in 1903 (a year after Bentley's death) architects and press alike were astonished by the splendour of its almost undecorated brick interior.[10] It was intended that the internal walls of the cathedral would be clad in marble and other fine stones when funds permitted, and some of this work was done during the following years. But above the galleries the great brick piers and arches fortunately remain uncovered to this day.

Westminster Cathedral was not the first work involved in a revival of interest in the Byzantine style during the 1890s and earlier. C. Harrison Townsend's extensive alterations of 1892 for All Saints Church, Ennismore Gardens, Knightsbridge, show the adaptation of Byzantine motifs typical of his churches. Only just outside London, at Lower Kingswood in Surrey, another Arts and Crafts architect – Sidney Barnsley – built the Byzantine Church of the Wisdom of God in 1891. But the cathedral's success spawned followers in many parts of Britain. Some of these were Anglican churches such as Beresford Pite's Christ Church, Brixton Road, Oval (1897–1903) and St Barnabas, off Shacklewell Lane, Hackney (1910) by Sir Charles Reilly.[11] More of them, however, were Roman Catholic. For just as the Nonconformists liked their churches to have a character of their own, Catholics welcomed the Byzantine style as one which would become identifiable as theirs through a long series of such churches built all over Britain during the following decades.

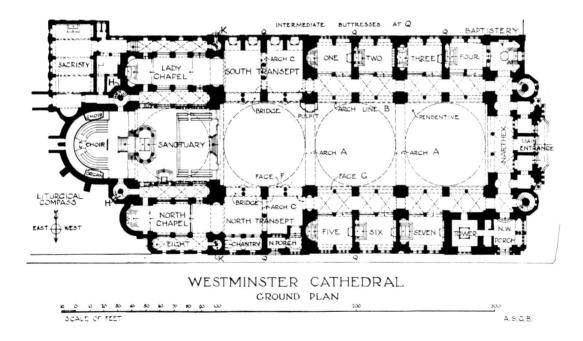

Fig. 153   John Francis Bentley: plan of Westminster Roman Catholic Cathedral (1895, first opened 1903, interior decorated later).

Fig. 154   Interior, Westminster Roman Catholic Cathedral, Victoria Street, Westminster (1895–1903) by John Francis Bentley.

13 Charitable Institutions

It is a remarkable fact that many of the most original London buildings constructed at the end of the nineteenth century were commissioned by private charities dedicated to improving the lives of the poor working classes. It seems that for social reformers of the time, the rejection of historical styles represented a symbol of their revulsion for any association with a past which had allowed so much suffering and hardship to grow in the midst of its developing civilisation. In 1891, the influential Arts and Crafts ideologist W. R. Lethaby wrote, 'What then will this art of the future be? The message will still be of nature and man, of order and beauty, but all will be sweetness, simplicity, freedom, confidence and light.'[1] Lethaby was a socialist of humanitarian ideals, like William Morris, and his ideas influenced the young London County Council architects (see chapter three) as much as they influenced those in private practice for charity buildings.

The importance of Church and secular charitable activities in the social history of the time is very great, but the story is complex. The social effects of industrialisation and the ruin of agriculture leading to appalling results in the slums of London have been traced in the early chapters of this book. The gradual relief of these conditions is rooted in political philosophy early in the nineteenth century, when Jeremy Bentham was questioning the usefulness of every human institution when set against the proposition that human existence is guided by the pursuit of pleasure and well-being, and by the avoidance of pain and suffering. Benthamite thought later divided into two main streams. One was devoted to complete self-help and developed into the free trade movement. The other believed that a 'tutelary state' was necessary to ensure that clashes of interest did not prevent each individual from achieving his own well-being. The second stream was the one taken up, and campaigned for, by Bentham's pupil, the great reformer Edwin Chadwick. Chadwick died at the age of ninety in 1890 after a lifetime spent meeting opposition and revilement, for he was a harsh man who made countless enemies. Despite this, Chadwick lived to see his beliefs adopted by a major part of influential British society. From these beliefs stemmed the attempts of government and charities to provide what he saw as the three major social needs – relief for paupers, health services and an effective police force – to overcome the classic evils of poverty, disease and crime. Indeed, widely accepted ideas on the need to intervene in the lives of the deprived went further than Chadwick believed proper and developed into Collectivism, the doctrine of collective responsibility, and the English forms of Socialism.

The efforts of non-government groups at the end of the century to improve the conditions of the poor in London were often confused in their aims. In particular, it is unclear whether the religious missions were motivated mostly by a desire to help

Fig. 155   The Penny Sit-up. Salvation Army hostel at Blackfriars (*c.*1900). For a penny, destitute people could sit up all night under a roof. They were not allowed to lie down.

people from Christian charity, or whether they offered help principally in order to gain souls for Christ. In 1900, *The Times* newspaper reported[2] a meeting of the London City Mission's 454 missionaries.

> Every missionary visits once a month about 650 families, or 2900 persons. The visits and calls paid during the past year number 3 385 472 of which 285 983 were to the sick and dying ... As a result of the year's work 5475 persons were induced to attend public worship, 1751 became Communicants and 562 were restored to Church Communion.

Fig. 156   Niven and Wigglesworth: Passmore Edwards Sailors' Hotel, corner of Commercial Road and Beccles Street, Stepney (1901).
Fig. 157   Beresford Pite: Ames House, YWCA hostel, Mortimer Street, Marylebone (1904). A layered brick skin covers the free forms made possible by the steel frame.

Other workers, such as Octavia Hill's staff mentioned in chapter three, were highly practical in their organisation of better housing in which Christianity shared importance with hygiene. The Guinness Trust employed the architect Mervyn Macartney to provide some good housing. And then there were Salvation Army shelters for the destitute such as that at Blackfriars – necessary at the time, although spine-chilling for us today – where people could sit up on benches in reasonable warmth all night for one penny. A purpose-built Salvation Army hostel was built by the architects Niven and Wigglesworth in 1905 in Garford Street, west of Poplar High

Fig. 158   Main entrance, Arlington House, Arlington Street, Camden Town (1905) by H. B. Measures. Hostel for single working men founded by Lord Rowton. The white-painted doorway was originally in unpainted modelled terracotta.

Street in the East End.

The poor were fed by charities, too. A writer in 1901 noted

> The scale upon which the Feeding Societies operate may be guessed from the fact that the Poor Children's Society at Borough S.E., instituted in 1885, provides nearly 2000 breakfasts and dinners weekly to the slum, poor and underfed children.[3]

And the Alexander Trust, founded in 1898 and supported by the tea millionaire Sir Thomas Lipton, operated restaurants for the extreme poor.

The commentator just quoted had much to say about contemporary workhouses as well. By the end of the century they were 'no longer of the kind described by Dickens ... The time has not yet arrived for such places to be strictly reserved for the sick and aged ... but they have vastly improved ... Workhouses are planted in every London district and all of them, with a few exceptions, architecturally as ugly as a Lancashire cotton-mill. They ... are all scrupulously clean – too clean, the inmates think – and perfectly ventilated, which to the infirm means draughts everywhere.'[4] This last comment refers to current public health and hygiene policies, a pre-occupation which we shall meet again in the chapter on schools.

The charities also intervened in the field of housing the poor. The Peabody Trust buildings have been mentioned in chapter three, but there were others. In the part of Marylebone around Great Portland Street, a number of hostels were built for the Church by the architect Beresford Pite. Pite was an active lay member of the evangelical Anglican 'Low Church', which kept clear of Catholic trappings and did much relief work in the slums. The very plain hostel called Balfour House, at Nos. 46–54 Great Titchfield Street, was built in 1896 with a pretty doorway decorated in Pite's favourite sculptured style. The next hostel, Ames House on the corner of Mortimer Street and Great Titchfield Street, dates from 1904 and was built with a steel frame structure. Here Pite restricted his decorative touches almost entirely to the brickwork, with high blank arches and diapering, expressing the frame within by tall canted bays which protrude from the block.

Simplicity of architectural manner was clearly suitable for charitable buildings both from a financial point of view and with an eye to their function. Notable examples of the inventiveness which architects managed within these restrictions include the Passmore Edwards Sailors' Hostel (now the Mariners' Hotel) on the Commercial Road in dockland (built in 1901 by Niven and Wigglesworth, in a grid-windowed Elizabethan manner) and the Rowton Houses. Lord Rowton started this series of massive hostels for single working-class men at the turn of the century and they still operate today. The Rowton House in Arlington Street, Camden Town (now called Arlington House) is typical of the huge austere blocks, with Arts and Crafts doorways, erected in such poor areas as King's Cross and the Elephant and Castle. The Camden Town building dates from 1905 and was designed by Rowton's usual architect, H. B. Measures.

If the charities cared for the souls, the bellies and the shelter of the poor, there were also those among them who sought their salvation by refining their way of life and aesthetic sensitivity. A contemporary account tells of the background.[5]

> The most remarkable of these philanthropic efforts, are the Settlements, as they are called, where educated men and women, putting theory into practice, take up their abode with the poor, striving by force of example to raise the moral tone of the district in which they have settled.

The most famous of the Settlements was and is Toynbee Hall. The same writer goes on,

> Arnold Toynbee, to whom it stands as a memorial, was an Oxford tutor ... He was one of the Oxford men who, between 1867 and 1874, went to live in the East-end, determined to see matters for themselves ... Canon Barnett (then the Rev. S. A. Barnett of St Jude's[6]) was the practical man who came forward to offer advice ... In 1883 he read a paper on the subject. His remedy was the University Settlement, the leader to be a man who had taken a degree, who was qualified to teach and endowed with humanity ... Toynbee Hall was opened in 1884, with a lecture-hall, library, guest and reception rooms. There are about fifteen resident graduates, either of Oxford or Cambridge ... In the lecture-room, knowledge, gained at the highest sources, would night after night be freely given. In the conversation-rooms, the (local) students would exchange ideas and form friendships ... There are East London people living almost as animals, whom the friendship of the more educated might startle into humanity ... there are in West London thousands who could supply the want.

A long list of Settlements follows, including 'the Passmore Edwards Settlement at Tavistock Place, St Pancras, initiated by Mrs Humphrey Ward (Mary Ward) and the generous Mr Passmore Edwards ... The University of Cambridge has taken charge of the vast population on the south of the Thames, as Oxford has done in the East-end.' Examples of the university type included the Oxford House University Settlement in Mape Street, Bethnal Green and, from Cambridge, the Pembroke College Mission in Barlow Street, Southwark. Here, the original hall is one of the rare London works of the extraordinary Arts and Crafts architect Edward Prior, built in 1892, but the

Fig. 159   Dunbar Smith and Cecil Brewer: Mary Ward House, Tavistock Place, Bloomsbury (1895–98). The design was influential on much of the early housing developments by the Architect's Department of the London County Council.

church above it was built by another architect in 1908. The Leysian Mission in the City Road, Finsbury (1903, by Bradshaw and Gass) should also be mentioned here as a Wesleyan Methodist Settlement.

The Passmore Edwards Settlement mentioned above is an even more interesting Arts and Crafts building. Now called Mary Ward House, it was built in 1895–98 to a design by the young partnership of Dunbar Smith and Cecil Brewer, which had won an eagerly awaited competition. Norman Shaw assessed the entries and the architectural magazines, if a little taken aback by the building, still welcomed it. 'The originality of the design is a little aggressive at first sight. But the originality is at least refreshing.'[7] The interiors are very simple, though there is attractive Arts and Crafts decoration in some rooms, notably the fireplace in the library. But it is the outside which is most important from a historical point of view, for its almost organic doorways, brickwork lower storeys and white-plastered top storey were taken up as the key elements in the frontages of many L.C.C. housing estates from Boundary Street of 1897–1900 onwards (see chapter three). The building is now used as a centre for the social services.

Another type of charitable building for the edification of the deprived was the public library. Many libraries were built in boroughs which could not afford to commission them for themselves, but these will be described in the chapter on education. Taking this idea still further, some wealthy philanthropists paid for buildings such as the Bishopsgate Institute of 1892–94 and the Beaufoy Institute in Black Price Road, Lambeth (1907, by F. A. Powell).

The Bishopsgate Institute brings us to the work of the most famous architect of London's charitable buildings, Charles Harrison Townsend. Townsend was an Arts

Colour plate 5.   Westminster Roman Catholic Cathedral (1895–1903) by John Francis Bentley.
Fig. 160   The Bishopsgate Institute, Bishopsgate, City (1892–94) by C. Harrison Townsend, photographed before the opening ceremony performed by Lord Rosebery, Leader of the London County Council.
Fig. 161   Detail of entrance, Bishopsgate Institute (1892–94) by C. Harrison Townsend. The decorative sculpture was Townsend's interpretation of symbolic links between building and nature expressed by W. R. Lethaby, the leading ideologist of the Arts and Crafts movement.

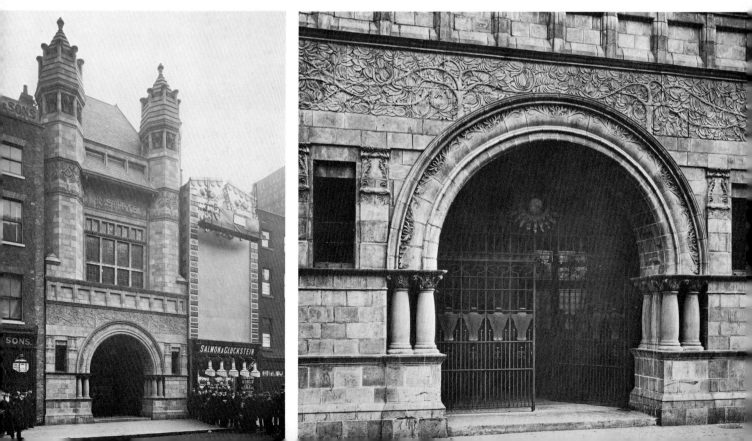

and Crafts architect much influenced by his own interpretation of Lethaby's ideas in the book of 1891 quoted in the first paragraph of this chapter. In an article of 1894 in *The Studio* magazine,[8] Townsend praised Lethaby's suggestion that architects should return to nature and ancient symbolism for their forms, emphasised the value of historical precedent (but not at the expense of originality) and urged architects to create 'common edifices capped at last by the soaring spires that sing their soul in stone'.

In the Bishopsgate Institute, which provided a library and halls for music and other elevating artistic entertainments, we can see an attempt to realise these architectural theories. Fantastic spires top a strong frontage which shows the influence both of Henry Wilson's church designs and of the much admired American free Romanesque of H. H. Richardson. The surface of the façade is richly decorated with sculptural relief in natural forms, trees whose branches swirl and intertwine. There are deeper underlying symbols[9] too, derived from Lethaby's book, such as the combination of a semi-circular arch with the overall square of the central window. It should be noted that the tendrils and curvilinear style of this type of Arts and Crafts decoration have caused some writers to dub it Art Nouveau. But a differentiation should be made between English work, which had its basis in social conscience and even in mystical symbolism, and the aesthetic approach of the Continental movement.

In 1896 Townsend designed a building intended, even more directly, to refine East End Londoners by bringing art to them. This was the Whitechapel Art Gallery in Whitechapel and both the unexecuted 1896 design and the design built in 1899–1901 show a continued obsession with circular forms combined with squares in elevation and in plan (a deep-rooted magic combination in all civilisations, according to Lethaby) as well as relief decoration with motifs drawn from nature. Unfortunately, funds were insufficient to execute the fine mosaic design by Walter Crane for the

Colour plate 6. The Horniman Museum, Forest Hill (1896–1901) by C. Harrison Townsend.
Fig. 162 Townsend's first design of 1896 for the Whitechapel Art Gallery. The mosaic was designed by Walter Crane. The underlying symbolism of the design was extremely complex.

central panel, or the two cupolas. It is worth noting that it was once again the formidable Canon Barnett who was the motive force behind the Whitechapel Gallery – Barnett had organised successful annual art exhibitions for the East End working classes since 1881 – and that Miss P. D. Townsend, the sister of the architect, was a close friend of the Barnetts.

The third and perhaps the finest of Townsend's major charitable buildings is the Horniman Free Museum in London Road, Forest Hill, south London, designed and built in 1896–1901. Without detracting from its originality, its developed symbolism and the splendour of its glass barrel-vaulted galleries, it must be observed that the contemporary Baroque fashion appears in various features of the great frontage. This time the large mosaic panel, by Robert Anning Bell, was executed and provides one of the building's high points.

The Horniman Museum was commissioned and paid for by another tea million-aire, F. J. Horniman M.P. His personal collection of anthropological objects grew so large that he opened it to the public in his home and then donated it to the London County Council in its new building for the enjoyment of the people. When one thinks of the impoverished men and women in the Salvation Army hostels or those chilled in the perfectly ventilated workhouses of that time, one may wonder whether the promoters of the Whitechapel Art Gallery and of the Horniman Museum had their priorities right. But it is comforting to reflect that these cultural centres have gone on giving pleasure to Londoners long after the workhouses and penny sit-ups have disappeared.

Fig. 164   C. Harrison Townsend: the Horniman Museum, London Road, Forest Hill, Lewisham, South London (1896–1901). The tower was a development of that designed for the Whitechapel Art Gallery, but was not executed.

Fig. 165   C. Harrison Townsend: interior, Horniman Museum (designed 1896, opened 1901) showing high barrel vault, and doorway capital decoration, now vandalised by proprietors.

Fig. 163 (*Opposite page*)   C. Harrison Townsend. The Whitechapel Art Gallery, Whitechapel (1899–1901).

14 Education, Libraries and Museums

According to the doctrines of Collectivism, increasingly influential in late Victorian times, direct action against poverty, crime and disease must be supplemented by educational services to enable children and adults individually to enjoy and profit from the possibilities of life when, in due time, these social ills should vanish. The *Education Act* of 1870 started this process by creating elected School Boards with responsibility for seeing that the nation's children received an education.

The individual classroom in London schools was an innovation which followed the new powers given to the London School Board in 1870. Writing[1] in 1874, the architect to the Board, E. R. Robson (1835–1917), pointed out that earlier schools usually consisted of 'a single lofty and noble hall of oblong form, in which the whole of the boys might be seen engaged in their various lessons – learning by heart or carefully plodding with grammar and dictionary – within sight of a master who was placed on a raised platform'.

Between 1871, when he was appointed architect to the Board, and 1884, Robson with J. J. Stevenson and some others designed and built 289 new London schools to provide places for over 300 000 children.[2] They introduced the new 'Queen Anne' style which gave these tall buildings their very striking presence in many localities of London, and they experimented with plans of great variety on the theme of classrooms around the central hall. The schools were extravagantly spacious for their time and the building programme had to survive many criticisms, such as the warning by the Department of Education in 1878 that it would not finance any more schools which cost more than £10 per pupil place.

By the 1890s the excellence of the Board schools 'keeping watch and ward over the interests of the generation that is to replace our own' was much praised,[3] and contrasted with the deplorable state of many religious and charitable school buildings. The Board's concentration on Secondary Schools contributed to the build-up of a generation of young people educated to the standards needed for the new clerical jobs created around 1900 by the expansion of central and local government activities and by the growth of insurance, banking and commerce in the City of London. At the same time, primary education had not developed so much and it has been convincingly argued that this recruitment to the middle classes was obtained at the expense of possible improvements in education for the working classes. It was only after 1914–18 that accepted educational theory ceased to discriminate between the standards of school buildings desirable for the different social classes. Before that it was widely felt that schools should not set 'an unattainable ideal ... making the child discontented with his home life.'[4]

In the early years of the new century, the important changes in school design were often brought about by doctors, rather than by educationists. In 1905, a deputation

Fig. 166   Girls playing Fives at Hampstead High School (*c*.1900).

of doctors to the Board of Education brought to a head the movement to pay more attention to hygiene in schools[5] and this resulted in a report on school medical inspections later that year. There were amendments to the Rules to be observed in planning and fitting up schools, issued by the Board of Education since 1900. One of the results of these amendments and of the new thinking following the *Education Act* of 1902 (which introduced a school leaving age and local government responsibility for education), was that the tall three-storey or four-storey schools of E. R. Robson were discouraged in new building. From 1902 onwards, the Board of Education Rules recommended that schools should be on one level only or 'in any case not on more than two floors'. Central halls were still advocated and boys and girls were still to be separated from each other. The Board's advice about the number of storeys was widely followed in primary and in suburban schools, but nearer the centre of London the price of land caused three-storey schools, such as Royal College Street School, St Pancras, to be built as late as 1910.

The new requirement for low-spreading buildings together with changing architectural fashion led to the abandonment of the 'Queen Anne' style of Robson and Stevenson which was typically vertical in emphasis. *The Education Act* of 1902 was passed by Parliament at the height of the fashion for Edwardian Baroque architecture in the new Town Halls and other municipal buildings, and it is not surprising that a rather charming, freely Neo-Georgian manner was widely used for the new schools built in the following decade. Good examples of the Edwardian elementary school, Pelham (1909) and Durnsford (1910, by W. H. Webb) Schools in Wimbledon, and secondary school, Hortensia Road Girls' School (1908, by T. J. Bailey, Robson's successor as architect to the Board) in Chelsea, are illustrated in

Fig. 167   Ainsworth Street School (1901) by the L.C.C. Architect's Department, on the Boundary Street housing estate, Shoreditch.

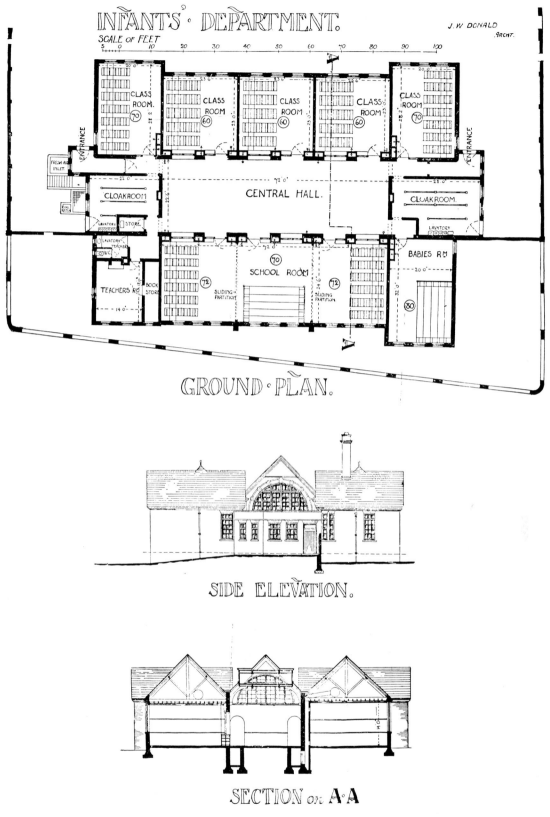

Fig. 168 Typical plan of an Edwardian primary school.

Seaborne and Lowe's *The English School* and can be seen today.

It is harder to find surviving buildings showing some of the more extreme results of educational theory in the years after 1900. Apart from the new teaching methods of Pestalozzi, Froebel and Montessori, contemporary American and German ideas were taken up in London after 1903 so that 'debilitated children should, through open-air schools, be given a chance to live, and grow, and develop ...'[7] Open-air schools were single-storey buildings with much-used playgrounds and a wall in each classroom which was made of roller-blind, to be opened whenever the weather made it possible, or was removable.

Apart from the open-air buildings, other private schools in London soon followed the Board School's use of the Neo-Georgian style of architecture. St Paul's School for Girls, Brook Green, Hammersmith was designed in this manner by an Arts and Crafts architect, Gerald Horsley, and built in 1904–07. It is a handsome composition of brick with stone dressing, quiet in its forms except for the high banded chimneys and bell tower over the barrel-vaulted hall. It has some pretty sculptural detailing.

In a similar style, the University College School was started in 1906 in Frognal, Hampstead, to the designs of Arnold Mitchell. It was opened in 1907 as a day-boys' Public School (fee-paying, for pupils aged thirteen to eighteen) by King Edward VII, whose stately statue now stands above its Baroque doorway. Sadly, the central block with its fine hall was gutted by fire in 1978.

Charity and church schools for the poor could not afford the same display as these private schools, but the planning and hygiene reforms of the State schools applied to them too and sometimes notable architects gave their design services free. A good

Fig. 170   Gerald Horsley: St Paul's Girls' School, Brook Green, Hammersmith (*c*.1900–04).
Fig. 169 (*Opposite page*) Royal College Street School, Kentish Town (1910–13) by the L.C.C. Architect's Department. The inventive Neo-Georgian type of design appeared in many L.C.C. schools after 1900.

instance is All Souls' School in Foley Street, a poor part of Marylebone behind the Middlesex Hospital. Built in 1906–08, Professor Beresford Pite's design cost little to build but his ingenious touches of Byzantine decoration and use of layered brick arches give the building visual interest.

Just as in the elementary and secondary schools, higher education policy still divided the social classes sharply. There were institutes and technical colleges for the lower orders, universities for those higher up the social scale. But that did not mean that colleges should always be mean in their architecture, for municipal pride was often involved and political feeling, too, in the poorer parts of London.

Thus, in the slums of Finsbury, the architect Edward Mountford was employed to design and build the Northampton Institute, St John Street, Clerkenwell, in 1894–96. It is a successful composition in a strong eclectic Baroque, still rather astonishing to come upon in such a bleak area. It is now the old building of the City University.

Even more inventive and highly decorated is the West Ham College of Technology (1895–98), Romford Road, in the working-class East End suburb of West Ham. Designed by James Gibson of the partnership Gibson and Russell, much of the luxuriant sculpture is in the Arts and Crafts Baroque manner derived from John Belcher's Institute of Chartered Accountants (opened two years before the design of the West Ham College). A similar Arts and Crafts inventiveness and charm, free from stylistic discipline, can be seen in the frontage of the Camberwell School of Arts and Crafts (with the Passmore Edwards Art Gallery), in Peckham Road, Camberwell of 1896–98. The architect here was Maurice B. Adams, designer of several buildings at Bedford Park.

These richly decorated buildings in a Baroque style which embraced many completely non-Classical features were typical of such London educational buildings until about 1905. The change after that is well demonstrated by another school in the Arts and Crafts manner, the famous Central School, Southampton Row, Holborn. Built in 1905–08, the specification for the buildings was prepared by the school's eminent Principal, the architect William Lethaby, and it was designed by a team from the L.C.C. Architect's Department led by A. Halcrow Verstage. Despite its stone frontage, there is an austerity about its rather strange style which reflects both Lethaby's own taste and, in more down-to-earth terms, the rising cost of labour and decoration.

In the wider field of public education, similar developments can be seen in the design of the numerous public libraries which were built at the turn of the century. The wealthy philanthropist, Mr Passmore Edwards, has already been mentioned in connection with the Camberwell School of Arts and Crafts. Edwards, Sir Henry Tate and the American millionaire Carnegie (who was of British birth) paid for the building of a great number of these London libraries. Making good books available to poor people was very much part of late Victorian reformers' ideas of enabling people to educate themselves and thus to improve their standard of living and quality of life.

As far as design is concerned, one of the most influential libraries was that in Ladbroke Grove, Paddington, built in 1890–91 by Henry Wilson, successor to the practice of John Dando Sedding and himself a leading figure in the Arts and Crafts movement with T. Phillips Figgis. Wilson's original design was compact and firm in its lower parts, but the skyline of the buildings was enriched with swirling sculpture.

Fig. 171   Main entrance, University College School, Frognal, Hampstead (1906–07) by Arnold Mitchell.
Following page
Fig. 172   The Great Hall, University College School. Gutted by fire 1978.

For economic reasons most of the sculpture was not executed, but the building still represents the wing of the Arts and Crafts movement which, decoratively, comes nearest to the Art Nouveau of continental Europe.

The end of the 1890s saw a stream of new libraries built in the inner suburbs of London, so that by the beginning of the new century an observer could write[8] that most boroughs had at least one, 'many of them being due to the munificence of Mr Passmore Edwards, who only last year laid the foundation stone of the new Public Library for the parish of St Mary, Stratford-at-Bow ... that has a population of about 50 000, the majority of whom are factory workers. As the Vestry (the local authority before the introduction of London boroughs in 1899) had not enough money to construct the library, Mr Edwards generously offered £4000 which was accepted.' This writer went on to note that there had been much scepticism about free libraries, for many people thought that books would soon be stolen. But in 1900 the library of St George-in-the-East reported only four stolen books out of 40 878 lendings, while Camberwell had nine stolen from over 500 000 lendings.

Passmore Edwards, who owned the magazine *Building News*, paid for several other public libraries in London, most of them designed by Maurice B. Adams or by Henry T. Hare. One of the most attractive is in Borough Road, Southwark, built with much Arts and Crafts detailing in 1897–99 by A. Blomfield Jackson. Another of the Passmore Edwards libraries at Pitfield Street in Shoreditch (1897–99), was designed

Fig. 173   All Souls School, Foley Street, Marylebone (1906–08) by A. Beresford Pite.
Fig. 174   West Ham Institute of Technology, Romford Road, West Ham (1895–98) by James Gibson and S. B. Russell. The Baroque revival at its most self-consciously artistic and most municipally proud.

Fig. 175   West Ham Institute of Technology. Interior of entrance hall.
Colour plate 7.   The Black Friar Public House, by Blackfriars Bridge (*c.*1903) by H. Fuller Clark.

SEIZE OCCASION

A GOOD THING IS SOON SNATCHED UP

INDUSTRY IS

Fig. 176   Passmore Edwards Public Library, Pitfield Street, Shoreditch (1897–99) by Henry Hare. A free and innovative approach to design by one of the most talented architects of the time.
Colour plate 8.   Dining Room, The Ritz Hotel, Piccadilly (1903–06) by Mewès and Davis.

by Henry Hare in a bold Free Style with eclectic detailing. Hare was one of the most successful architects of the time in the construction of public buildings in general, but he was pre-eminent in commissions for libraries. The dozens which he built all over England vary from the large and grandiose to the small and simple. In London he built the library at Shoreditch, two in Fulham (Lillie Road 1906, now demolished, and Fulham Road 1909), one in Islington (Holloway Road 1906) and one in Hammersmith (Brook Green Road 1904). Their chronological sequence shows a development through a Baroque style in the early 1900s towards a quieter Neo-Georgian by the end of that decade. Hare could handle any style with considerable talent, and these libraries show unremitting inventiveness and functional planning for the needs of their time.

The dominant feature of the public libraries was the Lending Department which usually occupied the largest area with a long counter for the public to take out or return books. The next largest space was taken up by the newspaper room, which was sometimes combined with the otherwise smaller magazine room, where members of the public were intended to educate themselves in current world affairs. Finally, the reference room and various offices completed the standard facilities.[9]

In passing, one extraordinary library of 1906–08 should be mentioned. The Carnegie Library in Thornhill Square, Islington, shows the eccentric architect Beresford Pite at his most original, in a style which he appears to have invented for the occasion, with Byzantine and perhaps even Celtic touches in the decoration.

Fig. 177　Public Library, Holloway Road, Islington (1906) by Henry Hare. An equally vigorous design by Hare, but now in the Classical manner widely accepted after 1900.

If colleges for higher education and libraries for public education seemed to the Edwardians to demand a fair amount of show, university buildings for the intended future leaders of the nation called for stately pomp. The twentieth century was to acknowledge that scientists had a rightful place among those leaders, and as if to announce the new order, the years 1900–06 saw the building of an immense Classical stone-fronted palace in Imperial Institute Road on the Kensington Museums Site to house the Imperial College of Science and Technology. The building was designed by Sir Aston Webb, the most prosperous architect of his time, who also designed the nearby Royal School of Mines in Prince Consort Road (1909–13). Webb's Classical buildings, huge and competent as the designs are, lack vitality and endearing qualities. One finds more human scale in university buildings of the time in the quirky brick Neo-Georgian of Basil Champneys' original part of Bedford College in Regents Park (1910–13) or even Charles Holden's undemonstrative Queen Mary's Hostel for the University of London, built in 1914 in Duchess of Bedford Walk, Notting Hill. Sir Ernest George and Yeates's rather overbearing Royal Academy of Music in Marylebone Road is a late example of Edwardian Baroque, dating from 1910–11.

Grandeur was considered the appropriate manner, too, for the major museums for the edification of the public which were built around 1900. While Sir Aston Webb was at work on his two giant university edifices on the Kensington Museums Site, work was progressing slowly on another of his big designs further down Exhibition Road.

Fig. 178   Plan of a typical small Edwardian public library, designed by Stanley Adshead (*c*.1903).

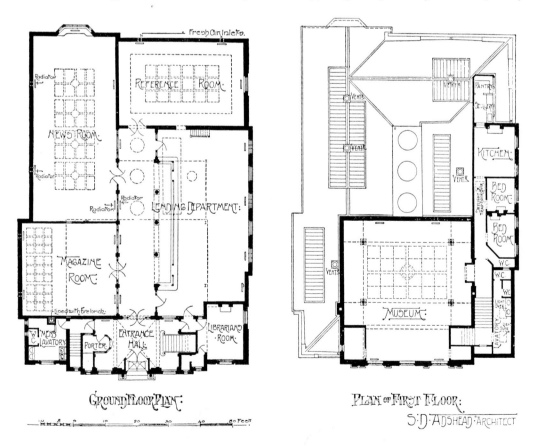

198

This was the building to complete the Victoria and Albert Museum. The design dates from the competition of 1891, as can be detected from the freely eclectic manner fashionable before the revival of classicism during the 1890s. The government finally found funds for its construction in 1899 and the museum was opened ten years later. The exterior, with its rather heavy forms and use of materials, must have seemed extremely old-fashioned in style to architects at its opening, but the sequence of imaginative spaces in the interior is one of Webb's finest achievements.

Soon after the competition for the Victoria and Albert Museum, another important public building started to rise on the site of the old Millbank Prison, which was being demolished. The Tate Gallery was built to house a collection of sixty-five paintings by English artists presented to the nation by the sugar millionaire Sir Henry Tate – these were valued at £75 000 and Tate contributed an additional £80 000 to the cost of the building, with the intention of starting a 'National Gallery of British Art'.[10] Tate employed his own favourite architect, Sidney R. J. Smith, who also built the public libraries which the millionaire had donated in Lambeth and Balham. The Tate Gallery, started in 1895 and opened on 16 August 1897, is in a Corinthian Classical style with a thrusting main portico which cannot hide the general weakness of the proportions and detailing.[11]

London received no national museums in the Edwardian Baroque style so popular between 1897 and 1906, but during those years the one major museum commission brought to the capital a refined Neo-Classicism of the contemporary French type. The King Edward VII Galleries of the British Museum (1904–14) were designed by the leading Scottish architect of the day, Sir John Burnet, after a limited competition. The Galleries are coolly planned and detailed, with a magnificent screen of Ionic columns along the street frontage in Montague Place, Bloomsbury. The interiors are equally restrained and refined and one may well regret that only this range of the Museum's plans for larger extensions was executed.

The final national museum of the period before the Great War of 1914–18 was the Science Museum of 1913–16 in Exhibition Road, Kensington. Designed by Sir Robert Allison, the building is an acceptable but unexceptional example of the Classicism which was to be typical of British public architecture during the post-war decades.

Previous pages
Fig. 179   Carnegie Public Library, Thornhill Square, western Islington (1906–08) by A. Beresford Pite.
Fig. 180   The Victoria and Albert Museum, Exhibition Road frontage, South Kensington (designed 1891, built 1899–1909) by Sir Aston Webb.
Fig. 181   The Tate Gallery, Millbank, Westminster (1895–97) by Sidney R. J. Smith.
Fig. 182   King Edward VII Galleries, British Museum, Montague Place, Bloomsbury (1904–14) by Sir John Burnet.

15 Services for the Public

Both the inventive human spirit and the increasing acceptance of political ideas of collective responsibility for the deprived led to a major extension of services available to the public at the end of the nineteenth century. Some of these services in London have been covered in individual chapters of this book. The provision of shelter for the needy was undertaken by local government and by the charities, as were other services such as education. But the role of private enterprise must not be underrated. The benefits of public transport and personal security through insurance around 1900 owed more to businessmen than to the early efforts of government.

It was business interests again that developed services such as electric lighting and the telephone, which started to grow just at this time. From 1900 onwards, the distinguished architect Leonard Stokes designed a series of telephone exchange buildings for the National Telephone Company, which his father-in-law managed. In the London area, these include the exchanges at No. 131 Lee Road, Blackheath (1900), at Nos. 57–59 London Wall in the City (1904), in Reform Row, Tottenham (1906) and at Kingsland Green, Dalston (1908). The best of all Stokes's exchanges, however, has been destroyed. This stood in Gerrard Street, Soho, where its dull replacement is still the local exchange. Built in 1904, the Stokes building was one of the most accomplished works of the English Free Style of architecture which flourished briefly at the turn of the century. But it must be noted that, in accordance with the Arts and Crafts emphasis on rooting original design in the local vernacular manner, the composition included many details developed from English buildings of around 1700 and this marks a stage in the spread of Arts and Crafts Neo-Georgian. Its combination of handsome doorways, indicating business prosperity, with the simpler grid of its upper storeys, hinting at functional efficiency, is also a good example of the architectural expression thought suitable in its own time for the provision of such a public service.

Despite the contribution of business enterprise, however, there is no doubt that the most remarkable range of new public services in the 1900s was provided by government, local or national. Again, we must look to the increasing belief in Collectivism to explain this. The Fire Service is a good example. With many crowded wooden houses remaining in the London slums, fire was still a frequent hazard. 'In 1899 there were 3846 fires in the Metropolis, over 216 being serious; there were 172 lives saved, and 119 lost; the chief cause of fire is still, as of old, the ubiquitous cheap lamp supplied with inferior paraffin oil.'[1]

The Fire Brigade was taken over by the London County Council at the turn of the century. In 1900 the brigade had sixty-five 'fire-engine stations' with fifty steam fire engines and nearly one hundred manual fire engines. The L.C.C. set about developing this service and many new stations were built by its Architect's Department (which inherited the responsibility from the Metropolitan Board of Works) during the next few years. The most famous example, and a notable work of Arts and Crafts architecture, is the Euston Fire Station, on a corner of Euston Square. Many of the young L.C.C. architects were active members of the Society for the Protection of Ancient Buildings, which had brought them into frequent contact with the older Arts and Crafts architects Philip Webb and William Lethaby – who dominated the S.P.A.B. – and, earlier, even with William Morris himself. The austere aesthetic taste shown overall in the Euston Fire Station (1901–02) is clearly influenced by Lethaby

Fig. 184   National Telephone Company exchange, Gerrard Street, Soho (1904) by Leonard Stokes. Demolished *c.*1930. One of the masterpieces by a highly talented architect, fitting his personal manner to a functional building.

Fig. 183 (*Previous page*)   The Kensington swimming baths in 1902, with boys learning to swim.

and by Webb's few London buildings. The high shape is emphasised by vertical accents. Areas of stonework and protruding windows give the frontages textural variety, while the detailing shows a severe Arts and Crafts elegance reminiscent of Henry Wilson or C. R. Ashbee.

Smaller fire stations at the start of the century sometimes evoked an almost domestic style, and another Arts and Crafts architect, C. F. A. Voysey, was evidently the influence in such buildings as that designed by the L.C.C. Architect's staff in West End Lane, Hampstead (1901). The stations at Hammersmith flyover, Clerkenwell, Old

Fig. 185   L.C.C. Architect's Department (Charles Winmill, Fire Section Architect). Euston Fire Station, Euston Road (1901–02).

Kent Road and Waterloo Road show the variety of these designs, for during the following decade these young architects followed most of the Arts and Crafts movement in adopting an idiosyncratic Neo-Georgian style for many of the fire stations and other public service buildings.[2]

Amongst the most notable of these public buildings are the police stations. The significance of these in 1900 must be seen in the context of the ideas promoted by Edwin Chadwick, as described in the previous chapter, and developed with much concern for individual freedom by other thinkers such as John Stuart Mill. The

Fig. 186   L.C.C. Architect's Department (Charles Winmill, Fire Section Architect). Fire Station, West End Lane, Hampstead (1901). A successful adaptation of Voysey's domestic manner to a public building.

Benthamite school's identification of the three evils of poverty, disease and crime entailed collective action against each of the three. Action by the State against pauperism grew slowly from the disasters of the Poor Laws and the Corn Laws towards the provision of cheap but good housing and later the dole for the unemployed and the *National Insurance Act* of 1911.

Action against crime was of course implied in action against poverty, for much of the one flowed from the other. Victorian crime was mostly theft, with drunkenness and street offences (such as obstruction) forming the other major types. The professional criminal population was low – the police estimated at the beginning of the century that there were only about 3000 'professional' thieves and perhaps 400 receivers in England as a whole[3] – and most offences were committed by ordinary working-class people or, in the case of fraud, by men and women from the middle classes.

The standard of the prisons had improved. Most of them were fairly old buildings put up during the nineteenth century, but the beginnings of a national prison service and standard can be traced from the *Prisons Act* of 1865. Before that there were 193 prisons in the country, and some conditions were appalling. By the end of the century this number was reduced to sixty-one, and the worst buildings had been demolished. All the same, it was a matter for wide concern that the number of people in prison, 167 000 in 1849, was little reduced by 1900.[4] This was partly explained by the abolition of two forms of punishment – transportation and execution for minor offences – but against this there was still a noticeable increase in crimes of violence around 1900.

Politicians and the public looked towards the police force for an even more direct answer to the evil of crime than education or the slow efforts to relieve poverty. In the nineteenth century the value of the police had been seen largely as preventive – by their presence and early intervention – but at the end of the century their role as detectives entered the public consciousness too. It was no accident that Sherlock Holmes became a cult figure at the time, as an idealised detective even better at the game than the professional police. The Metropolitan Police in London, 3000 men when the force was founded in 1829, was 5500 strong in the 1850s and 16 000 in 1901.[5]

Police stations were built rapidly from the late 1890s onwards, often with magistrates' courts in the same building. Under the force's architect, J. Dixon Butler (who had worked with Norman Shaw on the second part of New Scotland Yard, Andrew Saint points out), these police stations soon developed a very recognisable style of their own. This was a powerful Neo-Georgian manner, typical of its time in other types of building, but with some very particular characteristics. It can be seen as early as 1896 in the Croydon Police Station. Dixon Butler's almost Hawksmoor-like freedom with Classical detailing, and his love of impressive pediments used as gables or porches, is at its best in such works as Hampstead Police Station in Rosslyn Hill (*c*.1903) or the Police Station and Magistrates' Courthouse in Old Street, Shoreditch (1903). Despite the new police stations and recruits to the force, it is worth remarking that there was little difference between the number of people prosecuted for crimes overall in the 1900s and the numbers prosecuted fifty years later.

The third social evil identified by the Victorians, disease, also attracted attention and action at the start of the century. Public hygiene started to improve from the 1860s onwards with the building of London's main sewerage system. Mains water from outside the city was reaching more and more houses at the end of the century

Fig. 187   Hampstead Police Station, Rosslyn Hill, Hampstead (*c*.1903) by J. Dixon Butler.

and its quality was described in 1901 as 'clear, bright and well-filtered'.[6] Public baths and swimming pools were built increasingly and improved the standards of cleanliness. The death rate in London had been reduced to 20·4 per thousand by 1900, as good as any major city in the world, and it was only the remaining plague-spot slums that brought it above the national average of just under eighteen per thousand. The worst of those slums were being cleared by the L.C.C. (see chapter three) and further health improvements came with new standards of ventilation and drainage for buildings and the introduction of school medical inspection in the 1900s. Diseases found in children were often traced back to their homes and prevented from spreading – for instance, the inspections in 1908 showed that nearly one third of children were flea-bitten and the resulting campaign reduced that figure to less than four per cent during the next decade and a half.[7]

Although the terrible epidemics of smallpox, typhoid and cholera had been limited to rare local outbreaks by 1900, the policy of isolation to defeat disease was pursued by the growing health services for lesser contagious diseases, like the scarlet fever which could still kill whole families of children. Thus by 1901, London was

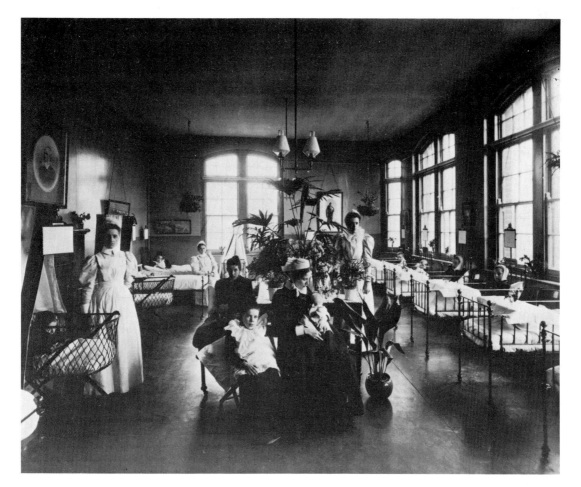

Fig. 189   Ward in the Plaistow Children's Hospital in the East End in the late 1890s.
Fig. 188 (*Opposite page*)   Detail of Police Station and Magistrates' Court, Old Street, Shoreditch (1903) by J. Dixon Butler.

GROUND FLOOR PLAN

fairly circled by a chain of fever hospitals, under the control of the Metropolitan Asylums Board. It has twelve such institutions, and two convalescent homes, providing, as it is hoped, sufficient accommodation to meet slightly more than normal needs.[8]

The plans of the hospitals built at this time were generally based on this need for isolated wards, their new features largely a matter of refining practice established during the previous decades. Thus Waterhouse's design for University College Hospital in Gower Street, Bloomsbury (1897–1906) has wings of wards which radiate from a central services block. In this severe building, as usual, Waterhouse (who worked on it with his son Paul) completely ignored all trends of architectural style going on in London at the time – the building could hardly be mistaken for the work of any other architect.

Another hospital, this time for a charitable group, was far more influential among architects. Charles Holden, who had worked with the Arts and Crafts master C. R. Ashbee in 1898, joined the firm of H. Percy Adams in the following year and soon took over most of its design work, which specialised in hospitals. Holden's first major design was for the Belgrave Hospital for Children, in Clapham Road near the Kennington Oval. Built in 1900–03, Holden's powerful exteriors show the influence of Henry Wilson and other Arts and Crafts designers. But the originality of the design is undoubted and almost overpowering, showing from the start a personal manner which was to continue throughout his highly successful career.[9]

The later part of King Edward VII's reign saw a further burst of hospital building. Holden's free Arts and Crafts manner was evident in some of these designs, but in many others, such as W. A. Pite's design for King's College Hospital of 1909–13 in Denmark Hill, Camberwell,[10] the manner is a rather grandiose version of the English Neo-Georgian style which became widespread in this field too.

So much, then, for the buildings put up at the beginning of the century as part of society's collective attempts to free the individual citizen from poverty, crime and disease. The changes in the organisation of local government to administer much of that collective effort, and the new buildings which resulted, will be examined in the next chapter.

Fig. 190 (*Opposite page*)   Typical design for a wing hospital ward by Percy Adams and Charles Holden (*c*.1905).
Fig. 191 (*Opposite page*)   University College Hospital, Gower Street, northern Bloomsbury (1897–1906) by Alfred Waterhouse.
Fig. 192 (*Following page*)   Charles Holden (as chief assistant to H. Percy Adams): Belgrave Hospital for Children, Clapham Road, Kennington Oval (1900–03).

16 The New Town Halls

During the 1880s most of the functions later carried out by local government authorities in London were managed by the Metropolitan Board of Works in relation to buildings and public works, the London School Board as regards education, and the parish vestries (predecessors of the boroughs) in other matters. With the inner London population still increasing and the conditions for the working classes and others getting no better, there were frequent outcries for reform and action by government at local level. In addition, the London authorities mentioned above were increasingly open to charges of corruption.

Yet among these unsavoury happenings, the outcome of one quiet architectural revolution was seen amongst the new vestry halls built during that decade. In 1885 the competition for the Chelsea Vestry Hall was won by John Brydon with a design in a style which was self-consciously English Classical. Town halls had been built in various Classical styles throughout Queen Victoria's reign,[1] but Brydon was intent on reviving the English Baroque of the early 1700s – the age of the late Wren, Hawksmoor, Vanbrugh and Gibbs – which he said was 'characterised by great vigour and picturesqueness, and by a freedom from restraint and an honesty of purpose not always to be found in later Classic'.[2] Brydon and others called this manner English Renaissance and promoted it as the new national style fit for the centre of a great empire. Thus the significance of Brydon's Chelsea Vestry Hall of 1885–87 – now the older part of the Chelsea Town Hall, in Chelsea Manor Gardens – was that it was one of the first buildings of the Baroque revival typical of public buildings around 1900, and particularly of countless town halls.

Other local government vestry halls of the 1890s showed a similar trend towards the Baroque, often with features of Elizabethan architecture mixed in. The Fulham and Hammersmith Vestry Halls (now town halls) reflect this tendency, and other good instances are the charming Battersea Town Hall on Lavender Hill of 1892–93 by Edward Mountford and Clerkenwell Town Hall of 1895 by C. Evans Vaughan. These were among the last halls built before the parish vestries were replaced by boroughs in 1899, for important political changes had been made during the decade after Brydon's design for Chelsea.

In 1888 the Conservative government finally yielded to the pressure for local government reform and the *County Councils Act* was passed by Parliament. The City of London's autonomy was left untouched by this and subsequent Acts, but the rest of London became a county, with a county's local government powers. A year later, the first elections were held with the wider mandate given to almost all working-class men in 1884, and the London County Council came into existence. The national political parties were not involved by name, but the first Council had a majority of

Fig. 193   A session of the London County Council about 1900 in the former Metropolitan Board of Works premises in Spring Gardens, off Trafalgar Square.

Liberals, including Lord Rosebery (the Leader of the Council) and Sir John Lubbock, and radicals such as John Burn the Socialist and J. B. Firth. Most significant of all, among those elected was Sidney Webb, one of the chief intellectual driving forces of the Fabian Society, which had been campaigning for Socialist reform since its foundation in 1883. These reformers and liberals grouped together with increasing organisation to form the 'Progressive' group in the Council, in which they held a majority until 1907. On the other side was a loosely knit group of 'Moderates' which included Earl Cadogan, the Chelsea landowner, and the Duke of Norfolk. The Moderates, too, formed themselves slowly into an organised party by the end of the century, and became increasingly identified with the Conservative party.[3]

The early meetings of the London County Council were held in the old premises of the Metropolitan Board of Works in Spring Gardens off Trafalgar Square. It was nearly twenty years before the Council finally started to build its own city hall. But its radical activities during those first years were the indirect cause of many other town halls being built within the boundaries of London. In 1891 the Fabian Sidney Webb published his manifesto 'London Programme'.[4] The Fabian proposals involved a massive drive for new L.C.C. housing and a municipal take-over of the trams, produce markets, hospitals, docks, and the water and gas supply companies – 'Water and Gas Socialism' as it became known. The Council tried to take up many of Webb's

Fig. 194   Chelsea Town Hall (older part, originally the Vestry Hall), Chelsea Manor Gardens, off the King's Road, Chelsea (1885–87) by John Brydon. Brydon practised and spoke publicly for the revival of the typically English Classicism of Wren and his Baroque disciples.

ideas, but plans for municipalisation were frustrated by the fact that they needed changes in the law of the land – and the national government would have none of it. It was 1900 before the first big housing schemes were completed (see chapter three) and 1905 before the L.C.C.'s first ambitious piece of city planning, Kingsway, was opened (see chapter one).

Indeed, the Conservative administrations with Lord Salisbury as Prime Minister were infuriated by the radical ambitions of the L.C.C. and resolved to prevent the Council from obtaining the extra powers which it had been demanding. A new Act was passed by Parliament, transforming the old London vestries into municipal boroughs in 1899 with new powers, including those over the personal Social Services – which the L.C.C. had wanted, with the intention of bringing about major social change.

For the building trade and architects the results were immediate. Many town halls had been built all over England following the *County Councils Act* of 1888, and the new suburban London Boroughs were not prepared to be outdone in their show of municipal importance. Before the year 1899 was finished, architectural competitions were held for the Woolwich and the Wandsworth Town Halls, and others followed soon afterwards.[5]

The competition for Woolwich Town Hall was won by A. Brumwell Thomas (later Sir Alfred) who was already building the glorious Belfast City Hall and was shortly to design the equally imposing Stockport Town Hall. Brumwell Thomas was one of the

Fig. 195   Clerkenwell Town Hall, Rosebery Avenue (1893–95) by C. Evans Vaughan.

most self-confident exponents of the English Baroque promoted by many architects after John Brydon's Chelsea Town Hall, and now widely known as Edwardian Baroque. The building of 1899–1905 at Wellington Street in Woolwich (now the Greenwich Town Hall as a result of later changes in borough boundaries) is one of the most striking products of the style. Its frontage is a highly ambitious Baroque composition of Ionic columns, round-topped pediments contrasting with a central pointed pediment and rising to a rather heavy dome. Above it soars a tremendous tower, with a bell-stage of exaggerated height, a usual feature of Edwardian town halls symbolising their new powers. The sculpture is good, but by no means as fine as the best examples seen in Edwardian Baroque buildings. The exterior departs further from the manner of Wren's St Paul's Cathedral than does Brumwell Thomas' earlier

Previous pages
Fig. 196   Woolwich (now Greenwich) Town Hall, Wellington Street, Woolwich (1899–1905) by Sir A. Brumwell Thomas. One of the splendid Baroque extravaganzas of the Edwardian era.
Fig. 197   The Council Chamber, Woolwich Town Hall.
Below
Fig. 198   Deptford Town Hall, New Cross Road, Lewisham (1902–05) by Lanchester and Rickards.

design for Belfast, but the interiors of the Council Chamber and Public Hall are emphatically like Wren at his grandest. The scale and extravagance of the building are extraordinary for a not too prosperous suburb of London.

One of the best of the Edwardian town halls is that built for the Borough of Deptford, in New Cross Road, Lewisham. This was put up in 1902–05 by another of the most successful firms of Edwardian Baroque architects, Lanchester and Rickards. E. A. Rickards, who was the draughtsman-designer of the firm, often drew on Austrian Baroque sources, rather than English, for his effervescent decoration and compositions. At Deptford, which is on a modest scale compared with some town halls, he is nearer to an English manner than usual. Both the exterior and interiors such as the Council Chamber show delicacy and a restrained inventiveness. It is one of the most charming town halls of the period.

Both the Chelsea Town Hall extension onto the King's Road, by Leonard Stokes, and the Lambeth Town Hall on Brixton Hill, by Septimus Warwick and E. A. Hall, were built in 1905–08 and still show the Edwardian Baroque style flourishing and at

Fig. 199   The Council Chamber, Deptford Town Hall.

Fig. 200   Lambeth Town Hall, Brixton Hill, Brixton (1905–08) by Septimus Warwick and Herbert Hall.

its most enjoyable. Warwick and Hall faced a difficult corner site in Lambeth and their solution is well planned, while the tower they placed at the angle forms one of the land-marks of southern London.

The Middlesex Guildhall of 1906–13 in Parliament Square is something of a stylistic oddity among municipal buildings of its time, for its proximity to Westminster Abbey caused the use of a Gothic manner. It will be dealt with in the next chapter, on the public buildings around Whitehall. Here, one other borough town hall must be looked at, for it is representative of many later local government commissions.

Bromley Town Hall, on the outer edge of south-east London, was designed by R. Frank Atkinson – who had built Waring and Gillow's store in Oxford Street – and dates from 1905–06. Its small scale suited its borough's budget, and the style is unmistakably Neo-Georgian rather than Baroque. The change in taste around 1906 can be seen in buildings of many kinds. There was a reaction against the flamboyant manner and decoration of the eight high years of Baroque architecture. How much of this was a purely aesthetic matter, and how much was due to the end of the economic boom, is a matter for argument. But both played some part. The result was that the extravagant style and costs of the English Baroque settled down into a quiet and equally English Neo-Georgian of much dignity. This did not happen suddenly, for some architects and clients continued to favour Baroque grandeur, but the Bromley Town Hall is a fair example of the new trend. There are Baroque touches at its main entrance, but the building overall shows gravity with little pomp in its brick walls and nicely detailed stone decoration. The Council Chamber is grave, too, with handsome stone columns and a restrained vaulted ceiling.

The same tendency towards restrained dignity can be seen in the winning design

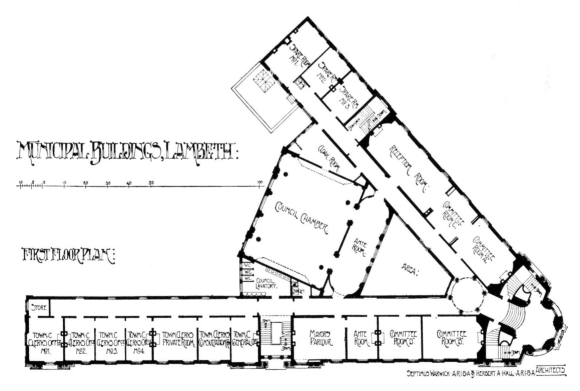

Fig. 201 First floor plan of Lambeth Town Hall.

for the County Hall which the L.C.C. at last decided to build in the middle 1900s. The offices of the various departments of the Council were increasing in size and were scattered around London. When the Progressives introduced the measure to buy the site on the riverside at the south end of Westminster Bridge, it was opposed bitterly by the Moderates on the grounds of wastefulness of Londoners' money. So successful was the Moderates' campaign that it brought them a landslide victory as the

Fig. 202   Bromley Town Hall, Tweedy Road, Bromley (1905–06) by R. Frank Atkinson.

Fig. 203 Competition design by E. A. Rickards of Lanchester and Rickards for L.C.C. County Hall, South Bank (1907) not built.

Municipal Reform Party in the local elections of 1907. For the first time they obtained power in the L.C.C. and they were to keep it for twenty-seven years.

All the same, most of the site was already purchased and the competition for the design of the building was under way. The result was announced in February 1908 and a comparison of the winning scheme with other entries demonstrates the money-saving mood of the new governing party. Lanchester and Rickards submitted one of their most amazing designs, very much in the public building mood of 1900. Rickards showed a richly decorated open screen-wall across a central recessed crescent, and a five-stage Baroque tower of curving lines rising behind a tremendous sculptured trophy at the rear of the crescent. The design was not given the prize, nor was an ingenious entry by Edwin Lutyens.

The winner was Ralph Knott, a young man of twenty-nine who had worked in the office of Sir Aston Webb and had built nothing himself. But Knott's design showed a keen awareness of the careful mood of the time among clients. It was a Classical composition of great simplicity on a grand scale almost worthy of Vanbrugh. Only the central crescent and a small bell-tower relieve the austere lines. There was a tremendous row among architects about the result, but Halsey Ricardo wrote in *The Architectural Review*,[6]

> Mr Knott's scheme–the best of them all–is a good beginning–a good first preliminary sketch ... But the majority of the competitors seem to have been so obstructed by the raging vortices of the conditions that ... there is no example of a fine inspiration.

The Moderate ruling party in the L.C.C. made a gesture towards their promised

savings by lopping off the eastern wing of the planned building and deferring the incomplete purchase of that part of the site. All the same, excavation work went ahead in 1909–12 and King George V laid the foundation stone of the actual building. The first part was opened in 1922, but Knott died before the building was completed ten years later.

So throughout the Edwardian period the L.C.C. continued to conduct its business from the crowded premises in Spring Gardens. By the time of the County Hall competition, the Council's powers had been increased by the *Housing of the Working Classes Act* of 1900, which enabled it to purchase suburban land for council houses, and by the *Education Act* of 1902, which gave it some control over the schools. Fire stations and swimming baths were added to the range of buildings commissioned by the L.C.C. or, through its influence, by the London boroughs. The *Town Planning Act* of 1909 brought some control over building standards and the use of land, and a little later George Lansbury started his long campaign for more pleasure-giving public parks and other provision for recreation. The figure of 10 000 new L.C.C. houses or flats for London families provided before the Great War started in 1914 would have been a disappointment to the Council members who first gathered in 1889, but as we have seen in chapter three, there were obstacles to quicker progress. Whatever the failures, the efforts of the L.C.C. and the boroughs at least laid the foundations around 1900 of gradual relief from the appalling social conditions suffered by many London people in Victorian times.

Fig. 204   The L.C.C.'s County Hall, Westminster Bridge (1908–31) by Ralph Knott. View from Victoria Embankment.

17 State Buildings – Whitehall and Buckingham Palace

In 1900 the buildings in Whitehall and Parliament Square were very different from those which stand there today. Many of the government offices in the neighbourhood were under construction at that time and the prestige of the area, from its nearness to Parliament and Downing Street, drew a number of other national institutions. The majority of the new buildings of that era follow the grand Edwardian Baroque style, the Baroque of the British Empire, but there were exceptions. Alfred Waterhouse, as usual, employed his tough Manchester manner in his Royal Institute of Chartered Surveyors on the corner of Parliament Square and Great George Street (1896–98), and the adjoining Middlesex Guildhall of 1906–13 is in a very free version of Gothic. This remarkable building by the architect of the Baroque West Ham Technical College, James Gibson, used Gothic decoration as a courtesy to its other neighbour, Westminster Abbey, on the south side of Parliament Square.

An early example of the Baroque in Whitehall is the comparatively quiet building of 1893–95 which Sir Aston Webb built for the Royal United Services Institute, next to Inigo Jones's famous Banqueting House (Webb was careful to keep his skyline below Jones's). Indeed, the R.U.S.I. is so restrained that only the blocked quoins and fashionable turret link it to the contemporary Arts and Crafts Baroque of Belcher and Pite.[1]

Another Westminster building dating from a few years later shows the Baroque in full glory. This is the Central Hall, Westminster, in Storey's Gate near the west end of the Abbey. The client, unexpectedly for such a flamboyant building, was the Methodist Church, but it was built to provide meeting rooms for any gathering which wanted to hire them. Equally unexpected is the inspiration of the Baroque manner which the architects, Lanchester and Rickards, employed. Pevsner's description can hardly be bettered. 'It might almost be a very substantially built Kursaal. French the metal dome, French the banded rustication, French the big square attic (a typical *Beaux Arts* motif), and French also the elliptical staircase with its bronze handrail.'[2] To this it is only necessary to add that the design by Rickards which won the competition in 1905 included twin towers on the frontage which added Rickards's favourite Austrian Baroque flavour to the French. The towers were not built when the Central Hall opened in 1911 and have not been added since.

So much for the non-government buildings around Whitehall. The major English Baroque edifices of the time in that area were needed to house the growing army of civil servants who ran the new services required to counter threats to the British Empire and necessitated by the increasing acceptance of social action as the government's responsibility. For if the State was to intervene more to defend its colonies from rivals and its citizens from poverty, disease and crime (see chapters thirteen to sixteen), it needed more employees and more money.

Fig. 205   The ceremony for the opening of the new main street, Kingsway, in 1905. King Edward VII is in the carriage on the far side. The demolished slum buildings can be seen in the background.

Government spending had been fairly stable in the Victorian era until the end of the century. The total national budget was under £70 million a year in the 1850s, but in the middle 1890s it rose sharply to over £100 million. In the 1850s there were 64 000 civil servants – by the middle 1890s there were 150 000.[3] There were no European wars during the period after the Crimea and the increase in spending went either to defend the growing British Empire or to finance government activities at home.

One of the largest callers for extra money was the Royal Navy, by far the largest in the world, which watched over the trade routes and the security of the colonies. Expenditure on the navy rose steadily from £10 million a year in the 1850s to £20 million by 1900. To service the growing fleet, the Admiralty in Whitehall was enlarged by a massive extension at its rear onto The Mall and Horseguards' Parade. The architectural competition for this building was won by the Halifax firm of Leeming and Leeming as early as 1884,[4] but it was 1895 before these new Admiralty offices were completed. The building has never attracted much admiration, nor does

Fig. 206   Middlesex Guildhall, Parliament Square, Westminster (1906–13) by James Gibson. The Edwardian free style in Gothic form is designed to blend with its neighbours, the Abbey and the Palace of Westminster.

it from this writer. It is a crowded composition, vaguely Baroque in its manner but with oddly uncomfortable detailing and a quirky skyline. It lacks splendour and it lacks repose.

The Army needed more London office space too, for its expenditure had risen from £14 million a year to nearly £20 million during the same half-century. In 1898 the government commissioned two major departmental buildings in Whitehall, one of which was the War Office. The architect employed here was William Young, who had designed the Municipal Chambers in Glasgow sixteen years earlier and had later cultivated an extensive practice among English aristocrats. Young was a designer of limited talent but strong conscience. The choice of an English Baroque treatment almost made itself, for it was the style of the moment in the heart of the metropolis which it symbolised. But Young expressed much concern[5] that the War Office should 'harmonise with its beautiful neighbour', the Banqueting House. His success in this aim, which necessitated making a successful composition around the ready-made

Fig. 207   Royal United Service Institution, Whitehall (1893–95) by Sir Aston Webb. A quiet version of the fashionable Baroque, to blend with its famous neighbour, Inigo Jones's Banqueting House.
Fig. 208   Central Hall (Methodist), Storey's Gate, Westminster (1905–11) by Lanchester and Rickards. Built without the two towers which Rickards designed for this frontage.

Fig. 209   E. A. Rickards. Detail drawing for Central Hall, Westminster.

plan which the government foisted on him, was only partial. But the War Office does have splendour, and its towers still serve as admirable focal points when one is going northwards up Whitehall. Young died long before it was finished in 1906 and the construction work was supervised by his son, Clyde Young.

The other huge government building commissioned in 1898 is, despite unfortunate alterations during erection, one of the best Edwardian Baroque works on a large scale. This civil servants' palace had no single department as its client, for it was intended to provide space for a number of expanding ministries. One of these was the Colonial Office, but their part of the building was subsequently occupied by the Department of Local Government and in later years by the Treasury. It was the civil expenditure on internal affairs which underwent the greatest growth during the latter half of the nineteenth century – the money spent on poor relief, education, health and public works stood at £10 million a year in the 1850s and rose to £24 million by the end of the century. To meet this and other burdens, the rate of income tax rose over a similar period from 4d. in the pound (1·7 per cent) to 1s. in the pound (5 per cent) in 1900. No wonder, then, that there was a need for the long Baroque building which stretches from the corner of Parliament Square and Parliament Street all the way to St James's Park.

The architect for this work was John Brydon, whose Chelsea Town Hall was described in the previous chapter as a seminal design in the revival of English Baroque. During the intervening years, Brydon had built a fine series of municipal buildings for the city of Bath, and now in 1898 the Royal Institute of British Architects recommended him to the government. Like William Young at the contemporary War Office building, Brydon had to work to a plan supplied by the

Fig. 210   The new Admiralty Buildings, between The Mall and Horse Guards Parade, St James's Park (1884–95) designed by Leeming and Leeming.

Office of Works, but at least he had a quadrangular site and room to set out a fine design, punctuated by Baroque towers, around a handsome circular courtyard in the centre. The concept is in the government office tradition of Somerset House, but the architectural language is inspired by late Wren rather than Chambers. Again like Young, Brydon died (in 1901) after completing the designs but before the building had even risen above ground level. After his death the government architect, Sir Henry Tanner, took over the supervision despite protests from the profession and made several adjustments to the design which detract from the clear articulation of Brydon's plans. The Parliament Square half of the government offices was opened in 1908 and the whole building was completed in 1912. The twin central towers on either side of the curving crescent at the Parliament Square entrance, distant descendants of the west towers of St Paul's Cathedral, make that long flank of the building particularly impressive.

While Brydon's last work was rising in Parliament Square, the Crown Estates Office of 1906–09 was being built to the dignified designs of John W. Murray beside the War Office in Whitehall. Further east, in the City, another Baroque palace was being built for the state, this time for the judiciary. The competition of 1900 for the design of the Central Criminal Courts on the corner of Old Bailey and Newgate Street, was won by Edward Mountford, architect of many town halls and of the Northampton Institute in Finsbury. By this time, Mountford had taken up the fully fledged Edwardian Baroque manner and the Old Bailey courts are one of the best

Fig. 213   The Government Buildings in Parliament Square and Parliament Street, photographed when the first half of the building was completed in 1908. John Brydon's design of 1898 was slightly and unwisely altered after Brydon's death. This part is now the Treasury.
Fig. 211 (*Opposite page*)   The War Office, Whitehall, Westminster (1898–1906) designed by William Young, who had built the Glasgow Municipal Chambers building in the previous decade.
Fig. 212 (*Opposite page*)   Grand staircase in the War Office, designed by William Young.

known examples of that grand manner. The design has its faults – the twin pediments of the frontage cry out for more projection to articulate the main entrance, and the disparity between plan and elevations was strongly attacked in *The Architectural Review* at the time.[6] The whole project was loaded with conflicting emotions, for it involved the demolition of George Dance's famous Newgate Prison, one of London's finest works of eighteenth century architecture, but a building described in 1901 as having, 'with the exception of the Tower, a record fuller of dark shadows than any existing London edifice ... forbidding and gloomy, frowning on innocent and guilty alike'.[7] Despite the protests of architects, the prison was dismantled and Londoners at least got a replacement of much dignity in Mountford's work of 1900–06, even if the architectural quality was not so high and the function only marginally more cheerful.

The height of the Edwardian Baroque period ended with the buildings just described and by 1906 a more restrained form of Classicism became widespread in new designs. Some exceptions to this rule still remained to be commissioned, however,

Fig. 215 (*Opposite page*)   Main doorway, Central Criminal Courts, Old Bailey. Sculpture by F. W. Pomeroy.
Fig. 214   The Central Criminal Courts, Old Bailey, City (1900–06) by Edward Mountford.

Fig. 216   Edward Mountford: the Great Hall under the dome, Central Criminal Courts, Old Bailey. Sculpture by F. W. Pomeroy, paintings by Gerald Moira.

Fig. 217 (*Opposite page*)   The Young Men's Christian Association central hostel, Tottenham Court Road (1911): architect nominally Roland Plumbe, probably designed by one of his staff. Demolished *c*.1970.

Fig. 218   The Port of London Authority building, Tower Hill, City of London (1912–22) by Sir Edwin Cooper.

and Sir Edwin Cooper's Port of London Authority building of 1912–22 on Tower Hill in the City (the Authority's foundation is described in chapter seven) has a central tower as extravagantly Baroque as any.

By chance, the Baroque style never reached the residences of the king whose name is so closely associated with it. Throughout Edward VII's reign, plans were being made and remade for a rebuilding of The Mall, the avenue which sweeps from Trafalgar Square to Buckingham Palace, as a memorial to Queen Victoria. As early as November 1901 (the year of the Queen's death), Sir Aston Webb won a limited competition and published designs for a big circular colonnade in front of Buckingham Palace for this purpose.[8] Webb was to keep the commission, but it went through a series of changes. During the following years the roadway of The Mall was widened and resurfaced to its present dimensions, and Webb's idea for a *rond point* at the palace end was executed without the colonnade. A large Baroque monument to Queen Victoria was designed and executed by Sir Thomas Brock, who was knighted on its steps at the opening ceremony. Just before King Edward VII's death in 1910, Aston Webb was at last able to build the big triumphal arch he had planned between Trafalgar Square and The Mall. But his designs had been mauled by the Admiralty, who demanded that the arch should contain office accommodation. In November 1909 *The Architectural Review* noted

> The removal of the scaffolding at the east end of the Mall discloses another pitiable example of national parsimony in Art. Only in our own land would a government be found to demand the combination of a Triumphal Arch, an office building and an official residence in a block both pleasing and expressive. The new building is neither ... no archway can soar to grandiloquence when crushed under a row of offices. It is time someone took up the cudgels for the architects ... What the government has forced the selected architect to do is now disclosed for all to see.[9]

Poor Aston Webb has attracted much of the disdain which this cumbersome but endearing archway has been heaped with since then. Whatever the faults of its Classical façades, its curving frontage off Trafalgar Square provides a dramatic semi-enclosed space before the arch gives onto the wide vista of The Mall (frontispiece).

The rebuilding of The Mall was rounded off in 1912–13 by a new public façade for Buckingham Palace itself. Again Sir Aston Webb was the architect, but the fashion for public buildings by this time was for a delicate and rather French form of Classicism. The old east frontage of the palace was the early Victorian Classical range by Edward Blore which had closed off the open side of Nash's palace courtyard. Blore's work had a rather heavy character and Webb's design of 1912 replaced it with the elegant, if insufficiently strong, front which is so familiar today. Whatever the faults of its individual parts, the overall scheme of triumphal arch, boulevarde, *rond point* and palace front, is a highly distinguished achievement of the move to give London a centre worthy of an imperial capital – and executed without undue swagger.

The delicacy of the new front of Buckingham Palace expresses much about the vigour which was lost from London public architecture during the years separating the death of King Edward from the inception of the great post-war buildings by Sir Edwin Lutyens, Sir John Burnet and others. It is fallacious to think that buildings and style necessarily reflect contemporary politics, but if ever the architecture of a short period expressed the character of its monarch, it was the public architecture of the decade of 1901–10. It is hard today to realise how much he was part of the

Fig. 219   Buckingham Palace, East Front, as it was before 1912 (designed by Edward Blore, 1840).
Fig. 220   Buckingham Palace, East Front (1912–13) by Sir Aston Webb, completing Webb's great scheme consisting of his Admiralty Arch, the widened Mall, the *rond point* with the Queen Victoria Memorial, and the remodelled forecourt and frontage of the palace.

consciousness of the British people, even in the years of working-class struggle and political demonstrations around the time of his death. His sheer enjoyment of life and of his official duties quite overcame most people's disapproval of the rumoured mistresses and the banker cronies. When he died, the sadness of ordinary people was more for the loss of his personal magnetism than for the death of a King. As a New York paper put it, 'There is no other monarch whom the civilised world could not better have spared'. A new King, George V, entered the palace. For Londoners in general it symbolised the beginning of many new things. For architects, the young King's name perhaps had an extra symbolic value for the Neo-Georgian architecture now soundly established as the national style.

18 Pointers for the Future

Looking back from the 1930s on his youth at the start of the century, the commentator Thomas Burke remarked, 'Through the Edwardian decade people did things. But those things were mainly a trying-out; we were not really in the twentieth century ... Departure points for change stand out, and among those I would set the underground railway – the electric tram and motor bus – the making of Aldwych and Kingsway – the spread of service flats – the coming of popular cafés and popular hotels – the opening of Selfridges – the new social amenities of streets and parks – the use of tarmac and reinforced concrete – the brightening of Sunday.'[1] Burke's list was largely concerned with the lives of middle-class people. For the working classes, for the building trade and for the nation as a whole, the Edwardian period marked the start of much more profound changes.

The arrival of the new building techniques of steel and concrete frame structure made little impact on domestic architecture – houses were almost invariably built with traditional load-bearing structures until the theories of the Bauhaus and Le Corbusier started to reach England in the 1930s. But the story is very different for larger buildings of all sorts. The frame structure was so much cheaper and left so much more space available than did load-bearing masonry that the technique was in general use in London by 1910. For the most part the frames were of steel (see chapter two), but some architects and engineers were experimenting with reinforced concrete late in the first decade. H. V. Lanchester, of Lanchester and Rickards, used the Kahn technique for all but the dome of the Central Hall, Westminster, of 1905–11, described in the previous chapter. A. C. Blomfield, son of Sir Arthur Blomfield, designed Friars House, Broad Street, in the City, with a concrete frame in 1906–08. And the old master, Norman Shaw, employed an internal reinforced concrete frame for the whole of his very last building – Portland House at No. 8 Lloyds Avenue in the City. It dates from 1907–08 and a contemporary photograph of the men at work on it seems to express their unfamiliarity with formed concrete pouring. Shaw wrote to Lethaby at around this time, 'Reinforced concrete ought to do a lot for us. What do you say to have a turn on those lines? I am sure we are doing no good at present.'[2] Shaw's building had a rather complex interior, mounting to a concrete dome, plastered within. The rest of the structure was of reinforced concrete piers, infilled with bricks, again using the Kahn system of trussed bars with angled wings. All that interior work has gone now, rebuilt completely in 1972, and only the stone façade remains. This frontage is not novel or exciting, for unlike the later Bauhaus architects, Shaw saw no reason to express the concrete structure on the façade. Instead we see a restrained Classical elevation of stone, as near to the Neo-Georgian style as Shaw came in any non-domestic building.

By this time Neo-Georgian was becoming widely established as the general

Fig. 221   Men at work on an early reinforced concrete building in Lloyds Avenue, City of London, in 1907.

Fig. 222   Kodak House, Kingsway (1910–11) by Sir John Burnet and Thomas Tait. Burnet's French-trained Classicism still shows in the temple-like frontage, despite the forms stripped of decoration.

English manner of the time, largely because of its acceptance by the Arts and Crafts movement as the country's only widespread vernacular and because of the campaign for it led by Sir Mervyn Macartney as editor of *The Architectural Review*.[3] The big house by Sir Edwin Lutyens at No. 7 St James's Square (1911) illustrates the simplified Neo-Georgian manner well, in sharp contrast to the earlier Baroque. In larger buildings, the new mood took various forms, from the so-called Stripped Classical of Sir Edwin Cooper's Marylebone Town Hall of 1911–18 to the austere brick and stone Neo-Georgian of Charles Holden's students' hostel for King's College at Duchess of Bedford Walk, Notting Hill (1914).

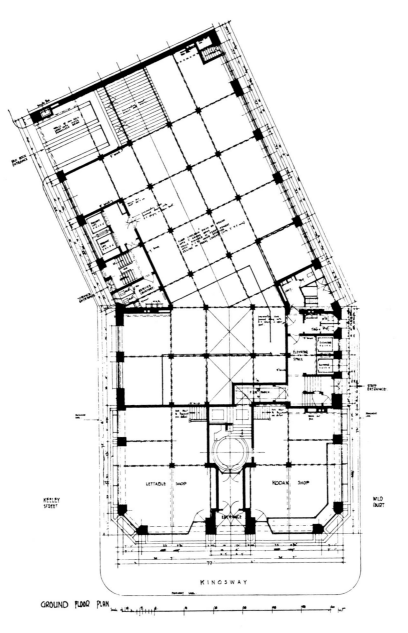

Fig. 223   Plan of Kodak House, Kingsway (1910–11) by Sir John Burnet and Thomas Tait, showing the freedom given by the steel frame.

Not all architects were prepared to accept the Neo-Georgian as the right style for London. Leonard Stokes, who had done much to develop the style at the start of the century, found it appropriate to do no more than hint at it in details in his very original office block of 1913–14 at Nos. 34–36 Golden Square, Soho. The experimental nature of this design is typical of the tentative essays of many contemporary architects to establish an external expression rooted in tradition but making the best of a frame structure. And Sir John Burnet, influenced by his young assistant Thomas Tait, produced an even more simplified office block for Messrs. Kodak, the photographic firm, in Kingsway in 1910–11. Further east, in the City of London, current European experiments with the same problem made an appearance in the big shipping offices at No. 32 Bury Street, built in 1914 to the designs of the famous Dutch architect H. P. Berlage. It still looks very foreign with its almost Art-Deco detailing.

Some English architects, too, continued to work in imported styles. Norman Shaw's fine English Baroque designs to replace Nash's curving Quadrant in Regent Street got no further than the Piccadilly Hotel of 1905–08. The shopkeepers objected strongly to the window area taken up by Shaw's massive ground-floor piers and between 1914 and 1930 the whole Quadrant and west sides of Piccadilly Circus were rebuilt by various architects working within overall façade designs by Sir Reginald Blomfield. Blomfield was fascinated by the elegance of French Classicism and his

Fig. 224   Regent Street's curving Quadrant in 1908, with only the new block of the Piccadilly Hotel rising above the level of the old buildings by John Nash.

handsome frontages are redolent of the Entente Cordiale and the alliance with France against German Imperialism.

For political events have some indirect influence on building, unpredictable and contrary and delayed though that influence often is. This post-Edwardian period was one of violent political change while the building industry went through a four-year period of prosperity before the outbreak of war. When King Edward died in 1910, Parliament was in the middle of the titanic struggle over Asquith's *Parliament Act* which ultimately deprived the House of Lords of its complete power of veto on Commons legislation. 1911 saw the equally contentious *National Insurance Act* introduced by Lloyd George, despite bitter Conservative opposition, to provide some financial security for the people. In the same year the major miners' strike was the culmination of the growth of the Trades Unions movement during the preceding years.

These events will be seen by some as symptoms of the internal crisis of capitalism at the time, by others as further steps arising from the wide adoption of political ideals described in the preceding chapters, whereby the State accepted responsibility for certain services to enable citizens to make the most of their lives individually. One of these services, of particular concern to the poor, was housing. That problem is with us still, but a considerable start was made in the years following 1900 in

Fig. 225   Piccadilly Circus and the Quadrant of Regent Street, as rebuilt to the designs of Sir Reginald Blomfield in 1914–30. The statue of Eros of 1892 is by the great sculptor Sir Alfred Gilbert.

providing new and decent accommodation for many thousands of London men, women and children.

Not all of those women were content any more with the role within the home which Victorian society had allotted to them. In the latter years of King Edward's reign, meetings were held with increasing frequency demanding opportunities for women to work in the better-paid jobs previously reserved for men. The question of votes for women crystallised their whole situation and the Suffragist movement split into those pursuing negotiations with politicians and those, called the Suffragettes, who took to open demonstrations in the streets and even violent gestures to obtain recognition.

Apart from these deep social changes, other developments occurred during these years which would change people's lives in a variety of ways. More and more people moved into the suburbs along ribbon developments as public transport in trams and tubes spread from the centre of London and the Building Societies arranged mortgages for new suburban houses. On the level of public entertainment, the movie house crept into city and suburb.

Fig. 226 (*Opposite page*)   St Marylebone Town Hall, Marylebone Road (1911–18) by Sir Edwin Cooper. Classicism stripped of most of its decoration.
Fig. 227   Dockers waiting for work, *c*.1900.

Fig. 228   Suffragist procession in 1910 in Hyde Park, with the first Suffragette to go to prison for women's votes.
Fig. 229   Spencer's airship on a flight from the Crystal Palace to Ealing: the first airship to navigate across London (1902).

In 1908 the movies were practically unknown to intelligent people. They were then shyly showing themselves in parish halls and in little fit-up places in side-streets of the poorer quarters, and were mainly patronised by children ... By 1915 the movies were everywhere and were everybody's entertainment.[4]

The electric trams and the underground railway were not the only types of transport which were developing. The motor car and motor bus were just starting their spectacular growth of the following decades and people were taking to the air. The first balloon airship flew across London from the Crystal Palace to Ealing in 1902 and by 1907 the Army had its own airship. And the aeroplanes were catching up with the balloons by 1910. London's first aerodrome was at Hendon, where a wooden shack was the ancestor of all the English airport buildings of later years, and in April 1910 the first flight was made from there to Manchester. In the previous year, the first flight across the English Channel had made the public realise the potential of air travel.

All this was heady stuff. But in 1911 there were more immediate and grim issues

Fig. 230.   M. Paulham leaving Hendon Aerodrome for Manchester, 28 April 1910.

needing attention. In that year Kaiser Wilhelm of Germany made a state visit to London. All through the Edwardian period, the threat of re-arming Germany had been growing. In 1900 *The Times* newspaper had reported,

> The Emperor William, addressing the officers of the Berlin garrison at the New Year parade yesterday, delivered a warm eulogy on the achievements of the army ... He would carry on and carry through the work of reorganising his navy, that by its means the German Empire might be in a position to win abroad a place it had not yet attained.[5]

His visit to London in 1911 was accompanied by reports of how far he had gone in making that promise good and his strutting, aggressive manner made an ominous impression on the people of England. Three years later those forebodings were proved justified by the outbreak of the Great War. For four years millions of men struggled and died on the fields of France and Belgium. During those years, which ended the Edwardian era so tragically, the building plans and the social innovations of the start of the century were put into cold storage. In 1918 they were taken out again and tested in a widely changed world.

Fig. 231   The Kaiser with King George V and the Prince of Wales (the future Edward VIII) during the German monarch's state visit to London in 1911.

Short Bibliography

Barker, T. C. and Robbins, Michael. *A History of London Transport*, Vols. 1 and 2 (London: 1974)

Beavan, A. H. *Imperial London* (London: 1901)

Belcher, John and Macartney, Mervyn. *Later Renaissance Architecture in England* (London: 1898–1901)

Belcher, John. *Essentials in Architecture* (London: 1907)

Blomfield, Reginald. *The Mistress Art* (London: 1908)

Blomfield, Reginald. *A History of French Architecture* (London: 1911 onwards)

Booth, Charles (ed.) *The Labour and Life of the People* (London: 1891)

Bowley, A. L. *Wages and Income in the United Kingdom since 1860* (London: 1937)

Burke, Thomas. *London in my Time* (London: 1934)

Brandon-Jones, John. *C. F. A. Voysey* (London: 1957, undated reprint of a special issue of Architectural Association Quarterly)

Clunn, Harold P. *The Face of London* (London: 1932)

Cooper, Nicholas. *The Opulent Eye* (London: 1976)

Davison, T. Raffles. *The Arts Connected with Building* (London: 1909)

Girouard, Mark. *Victorian Pubs* (London: 1975)

Girouard, Mark. *Sweetness and Light.* The Queen Anne Style (Oxford: 1977)

Glasstone, Victor. *Victorian and Edwardian Theatres* (London: 1975)

Gradidge, Roderick. *Edwin Lutyens* in *Seven Victorian Architects* ed. Jane Fawcett (London: 1976)

Hobhouse, Hermione. *Lost London* (London: 1971)

Howard, Ebenezer. *Garden Cities of Tomorrow* (London: 1902)

Hussey, Christopher and Butler, A. S. G. *Lutyens Memorial Volumes* (London: 1951)

Jackson, Alan A. *Semi-Detached London* (London: 1973)

Jenkins, Simon. *Landlords to London: the Story of a Capital and its Growth* (London: 1975)

Kaufman, M. *The Housing of the Working Classes and of the Poor* (London: 1907)

Kornwolf, J. D. *M. H. Baillie Scott and the Arts and Crafts Movement* (Baltimore: 1972)

Lethaby, W. R. *Architecture, Mysticism and Myth* (London: 1892)

Lewis, J. Parry. *Building Cycles and Britain's Growth* (London: 1965)

London County Council. *Housing of the Working Classes in London 1855–1912* (London: 1913)

Lowe, R. See Seaborne, M.

Macartney, Mervyn. *Recent English Domestic Architecture* (London: 1908) See also Belcher, John.

Middleton, G. A. T. (ed.) *Modern Buildings: their Planning, Construction and Equipment.* Six Vols. (London: 1906–07)

Midwinter, Eric. *Victorian Social Reform* (London: 1968)

Mitchell, B. R. with Deane, Phyllis. *Abstract of British Historical Statistics* (Cambridge: 1962)

Muthesius, Hermann. *Die Englische Baukunst der Gegenwart* (Leipzig: 1900)

Muthesius, Hermann. *Das Englische Haus* (Berlin: 1904–05)

Pevsner, Nikolaus. *Buildings of England.* London Vols. 1 and 2 (London: 1973 revised and 1952)

Pevsner, Nikolaus. *Pioneers of Modern Design* (London: 1960). First published as *Pioneers of The Modern Movement* (London: 1936)

Priestley, J. B. *The Edwardians* (London: 1970)

Pudney, John. *London's Docks* (London: 1975)

Robbins, Michael. See Barker, T. C.

Robson, E. R. *School Architecture* (London: 1874)

Rubens, Godfrey. *The Life and Work of William Lethaby* (London: forthcoming)

Ruskin, John. *The Stones of Venice* (London: 1851–53)

Saint, Andrew. *Richard Norman Shaw. A biography* (Yale: 1976)

Scott, M. H. Baillie. *Houses and Gardens* (London: 1906)

Seaborne, M. and Lowe, R. *The English School* Vol. 2, 1870–1970 (London: 1977)

Service, Alastair (ed.) *Edwardian Architecture and its Origins* (London: 1975)

Service, Alastair. *Edwardian Architecture* (London: 1977)

Shaw, Norman and Jackson, T. G. (eds.) *Architecture: A Profession or an Art?* (London: 1892)

Sims, George R. (ed.) *Living London.* Three Vols. (London: 1902–03)

Sparrow, W. Shaw (ed.) *The British Home of Today* (London: 1904)

Sparrow, W. Shaw (ed.) *The Modern Home* (London: 1905)

Sparrow, W. Shaw (ed.) *Flats, Urban Houses and Cottage Homes* (London: 1907)

Stamp, Gavin (et al.). *London 1900* (London: 1978, special issue of Architectural Design for an exhibition at RIBA)

Statham, H. H. *Modern Architecture* (London: 1897)

Summerson, John. *The Turn of the Century* (Glasgow: 1975) Reprint of a lecture.

Thompson, Paul. *The Edwardians.* A Social History (London: 1975)

Vaizey, John. *The Brewery Industry 1886–1951* (London: 1960)

Webb, Sidney. *London Programme* (London: 1891)

Notes

Chapter One

1. *The Times*, 1 January 1900, page 9

2. *The Times*, 1 January 1900, page 6

3. *London in my Time* (London: 1934) by Thomas Burke, page 7

4. See *A History of London Transport*, Vol. 2 (London: 1974) by T. C. Barker and Michael Robbins, page 2

5. *Abstract of British Historical Statistics* (Cambridge: 1962) by B. R. Mitchell with Phyllis Deane, page 19, figures rounded to the nearest 100 000

6. B. R. Mitchell, *op. cit.*, page 60 and *A Concise Economic History of Britain* (Cambridge: 1954) by W. H. B. Court, page 206

7. W. H. B. Court, *op. cit.*, pages 197–199

8. Apart from the earlier *Labouring Classes Lodging Houses Acts* and *Nuisances Removal and Sanitary Acts*, the statutes passed after 1880 include the *Artizans Dwelling Act* of 1882, the *Housing of the Working Classes Acts* of 1885, 1890, 1894, 1900 and 1903, the *County Councils Act* of 1888 (which brought the London County Council into existence in 1889), the *Public Health (London) Act* of 1891 and the *Housing, Town Planning etc. Act* of 1909

9. *The Builder*, 26 May 1900, page 507

10. An excellent account of the appearance of these fashionable untrained women designers of interiors in the 1890s is given in *The Opulent Eye* (London 1976) in Nicholas Cooper's introductory essay

11. *Semi-Detached London* (London: 1973) by Alan A. Jackson, page 47

12. Thomas Burke, *op. cit.*, page 65

13. *The Builder*, 5 May 1900, page 434

14. *The Face of London* (London: 1932) by Harold P. Clunn, pages 97 and 102

15. The best account of the Regent Street project is in *Richard Norman Shaw* (Yale: 1976) by Andrew Saint

16. Thomas Burke, *op. cit.*, page 202

Chapter Two

1. The phrase was used as the title for Mark Girouard's masterly book on the movement, *Sweetness and Light* (Oxford: 1977)

2. See *Edwardian Architecture* (London: 1977) by Alastair Service, pages 17–37

3. See *Pioneers of Modern Design* (London: 1960) by Nikolaus Pevsner, pages 106–107

4. See *The Turn of the Century* (Glasgow: 1975) reprint of a lecture by John Summerson

5. See Brydon's lecture printed in *The Builder*, Vol. 56, pages 147 and 168

6. Presidential Address by H. O. Cresswell to the Architectural Association, 1892, in *Architectural Association Notes*, Vol. 7, page 60

7. *A History of French Architecture* (London: 1911 onwards) by Reginald Blomfield

8. See *The Builder*, 10 May 1884 and the obituary of Belcher in *Journal of the R.I.B.A.*, Vol. 21, page 75

9. Chapters on Armoured Concrete by P. R. Strong in *Modern Buildings: their Planning, Construction and Equipment*, Vol. 5 (London: 1907) by G. A. T. Middleton, page 22 etc.

10. *Architectural Association Journal*, April 1913

11. See for example Ricardo's pieces in *The Architectural Review* of 1902, Vol. 11, pages 92 and 117

Chapter Three

1. *Imperial London* (London: 1901) by A. H. Beavan, pages 184–6. 3s. 10$\frac{3}{4}$d. was just under one-fifth of £1, while 6s. (six shillings) was three-tenths of £1

2. *Semi-Detached London* (London: 1973) by Alan A. Jackson, pages 41–44

3. A. H. Beavan, *op. cit.*, page 187

4. *London in my Time* (London: 1934) by Thomas Burke, page 29

5. *The Housing of the Working Classes and of the Poor* (London: 1907) by M. Kaufman, pages 1, 12, 70–73, 84 and 86

6. The earliest L.C.C. schemes to reach completion were the housing blocks built in 1891–94 in Shelton Street off Drury Lane (for 284 people, blocks designed by Rowland Plumbe) and those of 1893–96 and 1896–1901 in Cable Street at Shadwell in the East End. In Hughes Fields, Deptford there were cottages built for 666 people in 1893–95, while 51 cottages were built in 1901 in Trafalgar Road, Greenwich. There were also four housing blocks built for 418 people in 1896–97 on sites at Green Street and Boyfield Street in Southwark, and Boundary Street estate followed in 1897–1900. After that the amount of actual building carried out redoubled. According to *Housing of the Working Classes in London 1855–1912* (London County Council: 1913) these estates included those at Churchway, St Pancras (1900–02), Clare Market, Drury Lane (1899–1903), Baltic Street near St Luke's Church, Old Street (1899–1905), Webber Row, off Waterloo Road, Southwark (1902–07), Leather Lane to Gray's Inn Road, Holborn (1905–08), Nightingale Street, Marylebone (1902–05), Ann Street, Poplar (1900–02), Millbank Estate, behind the Tate Gallery, Westminster (1897–1903) and others

7. M. Kaufman, *op. cit.*, pages 15 and 28

8. *Housing of the Working Classes in London*, *op. cit.*, pages 70–71 and 125–130

9. *Housing of the Working Classes in London*, *op. cit.*, pages 72–75 and 131–137

10. Thomas Burke, *op. cit.*, page 207

Chapter Four

1. *The Builder*, 26 May 1900, page 507. For an account of the development of ideas about Arts

and Crafts domestic architecture and decoration from Ruskin and Morris up to 1900, see A. Service, *Edwardian Architecture* (London: 1977) pages 10–37

2. *The Architectural Review* 1903, Vol. 13, page 141

3. Magazines taken by numerous builders included *Building News, The Architects' and Builders' Journal, The Architect, The Builder* and *British Architect*, as well as the more art-conscious *The Studio* and the esteemed *The Architectural Review*. Books giving many house designs by well-known Arts and Crafts architects included *The British Home of Today* (1904) and *The Modern Home* (1905) both edited by W. Shaw Sparrow, *Houses and Gardens* (1906) by M. H. Baillie Scott, *The Arts connected with Building* (1909) by T. Raffles Davison, *Small Country Houses of Today* (1910) edited by Laurence Weaver, and *Modern Buildings: Their Planning, Construction and Equipment* (1907) by G. A. T. Middleton and other contributors

4. 'The Art of Today' by Voysey, published in *British Architect*, 18 November 1892

5. See 'James Maclaren and the Godwin Legacy' by A. Service in *The Architectural Review*, 1973

6. *Semi-Detached London* (London: 1973) by Alan A. Jackson is a major study of suburban growth in 1900–1939

7. *The Housing of the Working Classes and of the Poor* (London: 1907) by M. Kaufman, pages 18–19

8. *London in my Time* (London: 1934) by Thomas Burke, page 218

9. Alan A. Jackson, *op. cit.*, page 36

10. Alan A. Jackson, *op. cit.*, pages 71–77

11. *Imperial London* (London: 1901) by A. H. Beavan, page 144

12. A. H. Beavan, *op. cit.*, page 425

13. I owe a great deal to Robert Thorne of the G.L.C. Historic Buildings Department, who extracted an amazingly long list of Elgood's works from the Department's records. Elgood's office was at No. 98 Wimpole Street, which partly accounts for the quantity of his buildings in the neighbourhood, but he built elsewhere too (for example, see his flats in the following chapter)

14. *Architectural Association Notes*, 1898, Vol. 13, page 172. Elgood's paper was entitled 'Modern Architectural Tendencies as Illustrated by Contemporary Work'

Chapter Five

1. *Flats, Urban Houses and Cottage Homes* (London: 1907) edited by W. Shaw Sparrow, pages 16–17

2. Introduction by Verity in W. Shaw Sparrow, *op. cit.*, page 10

3. Introduction to *The Opulent Eye–Late Victorian and Edwardian taste in Interior Design* (London: 1976) by Nicholas Cooper, with contemporary photographs by Bedford Lemere

4. Detmar Blow (1897–1939) started his career as an extreme Arts and Crafts man, working closely with Edward Prior and Ernest Gimson. His Mayfair houses, probably arising from his association as architect with the Duke of Westminster's Grosvenor Estate, include 28 South Street of *c*.1902 and Nos. 45–51 Park Street of 1912

5. White glazed bricks are common on the rear elevations of Edwardian and later urban buildings. Among the buildings which use glazed and coloured bricks on their street elevations are Nos. 31–35 Langham Street (1901 by Arthur E. Thompson) and Radiant

House at Nos. 34–38 Mortimer Street (1915 by Frank Elgood and Francis Pither), both in Marylebone, as well as Debenhams department store and many tube stations. My thanks are due to Robert Thorne for information on the dates and architects of these buildings

Chapter Six

1. *Imperial London* (London: 1901) by A. H. Beavan, page 299

2. A. H. Beavan, *op. cit.*, pages 301, 303

3. *London in my Time* (London: 1934) by Thomas Burke, page 75

4. A. H. Beavan, *op. cit.*, page 304

5. *A History of London Transport* (London: 1974) by T. C. Barker and Michael Robbins. This period is covered in Vol. II, pages 15–191

6. Barker and Robbins, *op. cit.*, page 99

7. A. H. Beavan, *op. cit.*, page 298

8. A. H. Beavan, *op. cit.*, pages 287–294

9. *The Face of London* (London: 1932) by H. P. Clunn, page 223

Chapter Seven

1. *A Concise Economic History of Britain* (Cambridge: 1954) by W. H. B. Court, page 209

2. *Abstract of British Historical Statistics* (Cambridge: 1962) by B. R. Mitchell, page 60

3. *Imperial London* (London: 1901) by A. H. Beavan, page 187

4. *Wages and Income in the United Kingdom since 1860* (London: 1937) by A. L. Bowley, page 12

5. A. H. Beavan, *op. cit.*, pages 234–242

6. *London's Docks* (London: 1975) by John Pudney, pages 116–127

7. W. H. B. Court, *op. cit.*, pages 289–290

8. *Semi-Detached London* (London: 1973) by Alan A. Jackson, pages 41–44

9. Other office buildings by Treadwell and Martin in the West End include No. 60 St James's Street (1910), No. 106 Jermyn Street (1907), Nos. 78–81 Fetter Lane, Holborn (1904), No. 78 Wigmore Street (1906), Nos. 1–4 Spur Street (now part of Panton Street), Leicester Square (1909). I have to thank Robert Thorne for much work in extracting these dates from the L.C.C. minutes and elsewhere. Other buildings in Oxford Street, Euston Road, Mortimer Street and Pall Mall seem to bear the Treadwell and Martin hallmark, but the names of their architects are not established.

10. Elgood was architect of many houses around Harley Street (see chapter four) and of the big North Gate mansion block of flats north of Regent's Park. His lecture is reported in *Architectural Association Notes*, 1898, Vol. 13, page 172

11. *The Architectural Review*, 1910, Vol. 27

12. In a review of a book on the Royal Insurance Company's new Liverpool building, in *The Architectural Review*, 1905, Vol. 17

13. See *Journal of the Royal Institute of British Architects*, Vol. 21, page 50

14. W. H. B. Court, *op. cit.*, pages 323–5 and 334

15. *London in my Time* (London: 1934) by Thomas Burke, pages 230–232

16. The Bank of Scotland, Nos. 30–32 Bishopsgate (1896) is by W. W. Gwyther, the Australia and New Zealand Bank in Cornhill (1896) by G. Cuthbert. J. MacVicar Anderson, the Scottish architect (with his son) of the Waldorf Hotel and Australia House in Aldwych, designed the British Linen Bank (now Bank of Scotland) at No. 38 Threadneedle Street (1902)

Chapter Eight

1. *London in my Time* (London: 1934) by Thomas Burke, page 103

2. Thomas Burke, *op. cit.*, page 100

3. *Imperial London* (London: 1901) by A. H. Beavan, pages 179–180

4. Apart from the buildings mentioned in the text, the lower part of the Aeolian Hall at Nos. 135–137 New Bond Street (1904) by Walter Cave, Nos. 53/56 New Bond Street (1904) by W. H. White, Nos. 39–42 New Bond Street (*c.*1905) by E. Keynes Purchase, No. 44 Old Bond Street (1906) by E. A. Hunt, No. 180 New Bond Street (1908) by William Flockhart and Nos. 15–16 Old Bond Street (1911) by Charles Holden

5. *The Face of London* (London: 1932) by Harold P. Clunn, pages 385–387

6. Thomas Burke, *op. cit.*, page 98

Chapter Nine

1. *The Edwardians* (London: 1970) by J. B. Priestley, pages 155–156

2. *London in my Time* (London: 1934) by Thomas Burke, page 34

3. Thomas Burke, *op. cit.*, pages 155 and 173

4. *Imperial London* (London: 1901) by A. H. Beavan, page 471

5. *The Times*, 1 January 1900, page 4

6. *The Builder*, 17 March 1900, page 265

7. Quoted in *Victorian and Edwardian Theatres* (London: 1975) by Victor Glasstone, page 116

8. Matcham's London theatres include the Empire Theatre, Hackney, the Richmond Theatre (1899), the Hippodrome (1899–1900), the Coliseum (1902–04), the Palladium (1910) and the Victoria Palace (1911). Sprague designed the Coronet, Notting Hill (1898, now a cinema), the Hippodrome, Balham (1899–1900), Wyndham's (1899), the Cambridge, Camden Town (1901, now a broadcasting studio), the Albery (1902–03), the Strand (1905), the Aldwych (1905), the Globe (1906), the Queen's (1907) and the Ambassadors (1913). Crewe designed the Stoll Opera House (1910–11), the Shaftesbury (1910–11) and the Golders Green Hippodrome (1913)

9. Victor Glasstone, *op. cit.*, pages 98–133

Chapter Ten

1. 'The English Public-House' by Arthur Shadwell, in *The National Review*, 1895

2. *Victorian Pubs* (London: 1975) by Mark Girouard, page 10

3. Mark Girouard, *op. cit.*, page 181

4. Volume 1 page 163 of the Norman Collection in the Guildhall Library, quoted in Mark Girouard, *op. cit.*

5. The official objectives of the Central Public House Trust Association

6. 'Black Friar' by Nicholas Taylor, in *The Architectural Review* 1964, pages 373–376, describes the work

7. See *The Brewery Industry 1886–1951* (London: 1960) by John Vaizey, page 17

Chapter Eleven

1. *London in my Time* (London: 1934) by Thomas Burke, pages 60 and 177

2. *Imperial London* (London: 1901) by A. H. Beavan, pages 275–277

3. See *The Face of London* (London: 1932) by Harold P. Clunn, page 99

4. A. H. Beavan, *op. cit.*, page 453

5. Archer and Green also built the big Hyde Park Hotel in Knightsbridge, the Whitehall Court mansion block on the Victoria Embankment and the Cambridge Terrace mansion block on the east side of Regent's Park outer circle

6. Blomfield was writing his fine *History of French Architecture* (London 1911 and subsequent volumes) at the time and in 1907 was appointed Professor of Architecture at the Royal Academy, where he delivered a series of notable lectures, later published as *The Mistress Art* (London: 1908)

7. Harold P. Clunn, *op. cit.*, page 199

Chapter Twelve

1. See *The Edwardians* (London: 1975) by Paul Thompson, page 202

2. 'On going to Church' by George Bernard Shaw, in *The Savoy* magazine, January 1896, pages 23–24

3. *London in my Time* (London: 1934) by Thomas Burke, pages 148–150

4. Paul Thompson, *op. cit.*, pages 204–205

5. Thomas Burke, *op. cit.*, page 145

6. Quoted in 'Ecclesiastical Architecture' by Canon B. F. L. Clarke in *Journal of the Royal Society of Arts*, March 1973, page 234

7. Paul Thompson, *op. cit.*, page 204

8. *Semi-Detached London* (London: 1973) by Alan A. Jackson, pages 48–49

9. *Modern Buildings* (London: 1906–07) by G. A. T. Middleton, Vol. 5, pages 3–4

10. See *The Architectural Review*, 1902, Vols. 11 and 12, for articles on the cathedral as it approached completion

11. Most of these churches are outside London, but Dorothy Reynolds, who is writing a thesis on the Byzantine revival, has added to the London list, the church of St Peter, Southfield Road, Acton (1914) by W. A. Pite (brother of A. Beresford Pite, he otherwise specialised in hospital architecture) and of course the major Ninth Church of Christ Scientist, Marsham Street, Westminster (1926–30) by Sir Herbert Baker. The amount of mosaic work carried out around 1900 (e.g. the extensive mosaic decoration by Sir William Richmond and others of the crossing and chancel etc. of St Paul's Cathedral in the 1890s) is another indication of the fascination with Byzantine things at the turn of the century.

Chapter Thirteen

1. *Architecture, Mysticism and Myth* (London: 1891, dated 1892) by W. R. Lethaby, page 66

2. *The Times*, 2 January 1900, page 5

3. *Imperial London* (London: 1901) by A. H. Beavan, page 431

4. A. H. Beavan, *op. cit.*, page 199

5. A. H. Beavan, *op. cit.*, pages 428–9

6. The church in the East End, after which the Anglican church by Lutyens in Dame Henrietta Barnett's Hampstead Garden Suburb was later named.

7. *The British Architect*, 25 February 1898

8. *The Studio*, 1894, Vol. 4, page 88

9. For a fuller exploration of the symbolism of Lethaby, Wilson and Townsend, see *Edwardian Architecture* (London: 1977) by Alastair Service, pages 46–50 and 118–121

Chapter Fourteen

1. *School Architecture* (London: 1874) by E. R. Robson, page 235 of 1972 reprint

2. *The English School* Vol. II, 1870–1970 (London: 1977) by M. Seaborne and R. Lowe, page 8

3. *The Labour and Life of the People* (London: 1891) edited by C. Booth, contribution on schools by Mary Tabor

4. P. A. Robson, architect son of E. R. Robson, reported in *The Builder*, Vol. 86, page 308, in 1904

5. Reported in *The Builder*, Vol. 88, page 175

6. Seaborne and Lowe, *op. cit.*, pages 89 and 103

7. R. G. Kirkby in the *Journal of the Society of Architects*, 1909(2), page 403, noted in Seaborne and Lowe, *op. cit.*

8. *Imperial London* (London: 1901) by A. H. Beavan, page 425

9. See typical plans illustrated in *Modern Buildings* (London: 1906) edited by G. A. T. Bolton, Vol. 4, pages 1–9

10. A. H. Beavan, *op. cit.*, page 404

11. In 1910 a new Turner wing was added to the Tate Gallery to house the Turner Bequest, and the interiors of the gallery were largely reconstructed in a handsome Neo-Classical manner by an American architect in 1937

Chapter Fifteen

1. *Imperial London* (London: 1901) by A. H. Beavan, page 315

2. The head architect of the L.C.C. Architect's Department, Fire Section, was Charles Winmill (1865–1945). Winmill himself designed the Fire Station in Eton Avenue, Hampstead (1914–15), but research has not yet shown which designers were responsible for the other individual fire stations. It appears that some of the buildings were done by design teams. See 'The Architect's Department of the L.C.C. 1888–1914' by A. Service in *Edwardian Architecture and its Origins* (London: 1975) pages 406–411

3. *The Edwardians* (London: 1975) by Paul Thompson, page 196

4. *Victorian Social Reform* (London: 1968) by Eric Midwinter, pages 42 and 58

5. A. H. Beavan, *op. cit.*, page 167

6. A. H. Beavan, *op. cit.*, page 191

7. Paul Thompson, *op. cit.*, page 288

8. A. H. Beavan, *op. cit.*, page 199

9. See *Edwardian Architecture* (London: 1977) by A. Service, pages 109–113

10. The entrance block of King's College Hospital was added by Stanley Hamp of Collcutt and Hamp in 1937, in a very different, almost jazzy, Neo-Georgian

Chapter Sixteen

1. See *Edwardian Architecture* (London: 1977) by A. Service, page 60

2. Brydon's lecture of February 1889 is printed in *The Builder*, Vol. 56, pages 147 and 168

3. A good account of the early years of the L.C.C. is given in *Landlords to London: the story of a capital and its growth* (London: 1975) by Simon Jenkins, pages 191–197

4. *London Programme* (London: 1891) by Sidney Webb

5. See the *British Architect*, 17 November 1899 for Woolwich (referred to as Plumstead Municipal Buildings at the time), 29 December 1899 for Wandsworth, 23 February 1900 for Hendon, and 31 October 1902 for Deptford

6. *The Architectural Review*, 1908, Vol. 23, pages 156–160

Chapter Seventeen

1. Belcher and Pite's Institute of Chartered Accountants of 1888–93, in the City, was completed in the year Webb designed the R.U.S.I. and is an obvious influence (see chapter two of this book)

2. The Buildings of England, *London Vol. I* (London: revised edition 1973) by Nikolaus Pevsner, page 502

3. *Abstract of British Historical Statistics* (Cambridge: 1962) by B. R. Mitchell and Phyllis Deane, page 60

4. See *The British Architect*, 9 August 1884

5. See *Edwardian Architecture* (London: 1977) by A. Service, page 148

6. *The Architectural Review*, 1900, Vol. 8, page 3

7. *Imperial London* (London: 1901) by A. H. Beavan, page 170

8. See *The British Architect*, 8 November 1901

9. *The Architectural Review*, 1909, Vol. 26, page 224

Chapter Eighteen

1. *London in my Time* (London: 1934) by Thomas Burke, pages 16–18

2. *Richard Norman Shaw* (Yale: 1976) by Andrew Saint, page 393 and *Philip Webb and his Work* (London: 1935) by W. R. Lethaby, page 77

3. See the regular series 'The Practical Exemplar of Architecture' in *The Architectural Review* from April 1906 onwards

4. Thomas Burke, *op. cit.*, page 141

5. *The Times*, 2 January 1900, page 7

Index

Italicised references denote illustrations in the text